1000 PHOTOS of AQUARIUM FISH

Text and Photos:

Marie-Paule and Christian Piednoir

To Florent…

BARRON'S

CONTENTS

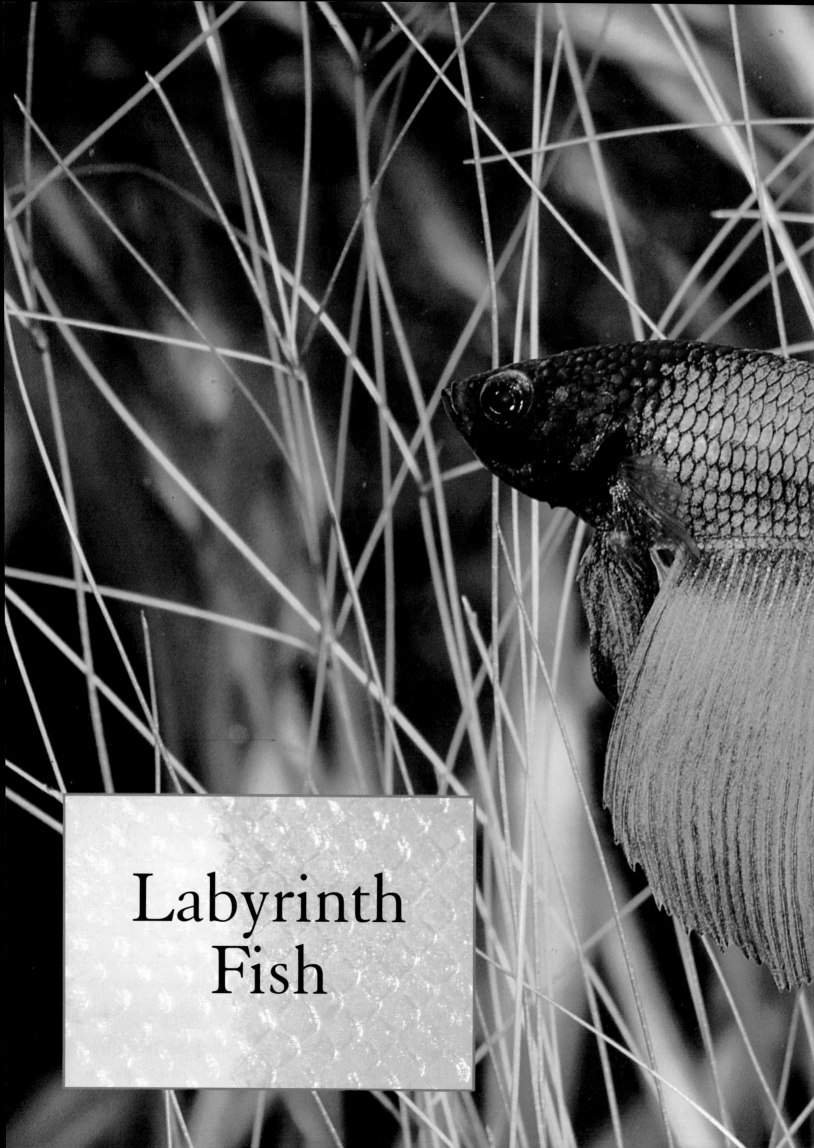

Labyrinth
Fish

Bettas and Paradise Fish

▲ Betta unimaculata *is a good jumper. It lives in fast-flowing streams and requires acid water to breed successfully.*

▼ *A beautiful show-quality double-tail betta (Betta splendens). Its caudal is divided into two veil-like lobes of equal size.*

Labyrinth fish are notable for having two distinct modes of respiration, the second serving to supplement the gills, which are more or less atrophied in some species. Native to the fresh waters of Asia and Africa, they are usually found in very warm—and consequently oxygen-poor—habitats. To more efficiently trap precious molecules of oxygen, these fish have evolved a supplementary organ of respiration supported by the gill arches, the labyrinth. Good aquarium husbandry of these fish mandates keeping their aquarium tightly covered, so that air and water temperatures can remain close to one another. Too great a difference can have fatal consequences. Although somewhat delicate in this regard, the species commonly offered for sale are charming additions to a home aquarium. Despite their appeal, some species must be banned from a community aquarium. In particular, representatives of the genus *Channa* are formidable predators.

Labyrinth fish breed in two quite different ways. Some species construct a nest of mucus-coated bubbles for their eggs; others are mouth-brooders, carrying the eggs in their buccal cavity. As a rule, the male plays the dominant role in the reproductive process. Whether building a bubble nest or carrying the eggs, he is clearly in charge.

The Siamese fighting fish is probably one of the best-known aquarium fish. Its many domesticated varieties have made it a best-seller among fish fanciers. It was originally a rather nondescript fish, with neither its red and blue coloration nor its finnage out of the ordinary. Breeders have succeeded in increasing the size of the fins and fixing a wide range of colors. Standards have been developed for color saturation and fin shape (when fully spread, the ideal tail fin should transect a 180° angle).

Although they are officially banned, staged fights between paired male fighting fish are still widespread in Thailand. Fins in tatters and lips torn, each is consigned to a small container, where, if his wounds are not too serious, he may eventually regain his health. You should now understand why housing two males in the same aquarium is inadvisable.

There are both bubble nest-building and male mouthbrooding Betta species. These fish range in size from the 2-in (5-cm) *Betta imbellis* to the 6-in (15-cm) *Betta macropthalma*. Bettas can be found from Thailand south to the major islands of Indonesia.

Paradise fish are closely related to bettas. They grow to 4 in (10 cm) long and have a more restricted distribution, ranging from northern China to Vietnam.

▲ *A young pair of* Betta pugnax pinang, *captured at Ipoh in Malaysia. Adults reach a length of 5 in (12 cm).*

▼ *Brown's dwarf red betta (Betta brownorum)* closely resembles Betta coccina.

▲ *This show fish, the product of many years of selective breeding, is known as a butterfly betta. It is a delight to the eye.*

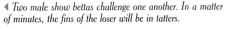
◀ Two male show bettas challenge one another. In a matter of minutes, the fins of the loser will be in tatters.

▼ Before the contest, the cardboard barrier is removed. The hostility of the prospective combatants, who cannot tolerate each other's proximity even when separated by a glass barrier, is immediately evident.

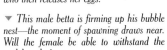

▲ Egg laying beneath a bubble nest by a pair of small Betta imbellis. The male curves his body around that of his consort, who then releases her eggs.

▼ This male betta is firming up his bubble nest—the moment of spawning draws near. Will the female be able to withstand the male's ardor?

▲ A betta breeder's stall in the Bangkok market. One fish per bottle, the bottles separated by a piece of cardboard.

▲ This female Siamese fighting fish is ready to spawn; her white ovipositor is clearly visible.

▲ The Javanese fighting fish (Betta picta) is one of the smallest mouthbrooding bettas.

▼ A commercially bred example of the domesticated form of the Siamese fighting fish (Betta splendens), best known of the bettas. Here, a solid red male spreads his fins.

▲ Male round-tailed paradise fish (Macropodus ocellatus) spreads his fins in an attempt to intimidate his own reflection in the glass wall of his aquarium. This species can withstand temperatures from 50 to 86°F (10 to 30°C).

▶ During the spawning act, the female Macropodus ocellatus becomes very pale. Embraced by her mate, she releases several eggs into this bubble nest.

▼ The black paradise fish (Macropodus concolor) was one of the first species to be imported as an aquarium fish, over a century ago.

▶ *The pearl gourami (Trichogaster leeri), among the most majestic of all aquarium fish and one of the species most popular with tropical fish fanciers. The two males in the foreground are courting the same female.*

▼ *The giant gourami (Colisa fasciata) is the largest species of the genus, growing to 4 in (10 cm). It is frequently confused with the thick-lipped gourami.*

Colisa and *Trichogaster*–Threadfin Gouramis

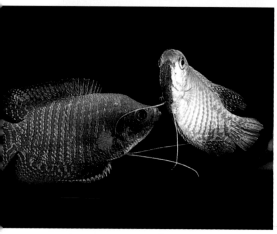

▲ *An aggressive encounter between two males of the wild color form of the dwarf gourami (Colisa lalia).*

The gouramis of the genera *Colisa* and *Trichogaster* are noted for their long, threadlike ventral fins. Chiefly organs of touch, their "antennas" are also endowed with organs similar to our taste buds. In an aquarium, two or three antagonists flail at each other with their ventral fins. These encounters may be motivated by courtship, a desire to dominate, or simple curiosity.

Colisa is native to the fresh waters of India and Burma and comprises four species, *Colisa lalia* being the best known. Its brilliant artificially selected color forms are highly prized. At 2 in (5 cm) long, *Colisa sota* is the smallest species of the genus, while *Colisa fasciata* can reach a length of 4 in (12 cm). *Trichogaster* species grow somewhat larger—from 4 to 6 in (10 to 15 cm) long and range from Thailand through the major islands of Indonesia.

The most popular species of the genus is the pearl gourami, *Tricogaster leeri*. It is important to house this species in a well-planted aquarium with suitable hiding places. A layer of floating plants helps these fish construct the bubble nest they require for spawning. Do not keep these gouramis with fast-moving tankmates! Barbs, in particular, are notorious for chewing up their threadlike ventral fins.

While spawning under aquarium conditions is triggered by temperatures of 83 to 86°F (28 to 30°C), water temperatures in the shallows of their native swamps can climb as high as 95°F (35°C).

Hormones and Breeding

This female dwarf gourami, well fed on mosquito larvae, will soon be ripe with eggs. This species breeds in any quiet, well-planted aquarium. Live foods provide fish with the vitamins necessary to produce the hormones that control the maturation of their gonads.

▲ *A color variety created by selective breeding, the neon dwarf gourami (Colisa lalia).*

▼ The luminous appearance of the moonlight gourami (Trichogaster microlepis) is due to its minuscule, highly reflected scales. This species is shown best in a well-planted tank.

▲ A nocturnal display by two males of another artificially selected color form of the dwarf gourami, the peacock.

▶ A selectively bred color form of the blue gourami, the Cosby is notable for its pattern of dark lateral blotches.

▲ Smaller than Colisa fasciata, the thick-lipped gourami (Colisa labiosa) also differs from it in its rounded anal fin.

▲ One of the color forms of Trichogaster trichopterus, the blue or Sumatra gourami. Prospective pairs get acquainted by stroking each other with the tips of their threadlike ventral fins.

▼ Closely related to the dwarf gourami, the male honey dwarf gourami (Colisa sota) differs from it in its orange coloration.

▲ The golden gourami is another artificially selected color form of Trichogaster trichopterus. It does not get along with the Cosby gourami.

◀ Less colorful than its congeners and thus seldom offered for sale, the snakeskin gourami (Trichogaster pectoralis) is the least popular Trichogaster species.

▼ The male dwarf gourami constructs a bubble nest, a project that requires much effort. Pieces of floating plants serve to reinforce this structure.

▲ The female honey gourami is easily recognized, but males in poor condition can present much the same appearance.

▶ *Native to the Congo River, the panther bushfish (Ctenopoma acutirostre) is a shy predator that can grow to a length of 6 in (15 cm).*

▲ *The kissing gourami (Helostoma temminckii) in is wild color pattern of olive green traversed by dark horizontal stripes.*

▲ *An adult combtail (Belontia signata), sometimes called the Ceylon paradise fish, can grow to 6 in (15 cm) long. Both parents guard the eggs and later the young.*

▼ *The leaf fish (Monocirrhus polyacanthus) lets itself be carried along at the whim of the current to approach its prey without being detected.*

Other Labyrinth Fish

Ranging in size from the 1 in (2.5 cm) of the smallest Parosphromenus species to the 3 ft (1 m) of *Osphromenus gorami* or the 4 ft (1.2 m) and 45 lbs (20 kg) of *Channa micropeltes*, labyrinth fish display a remarkable degree of diversity. The giant *Channa* species occur in many habitats. Some can be found in tropical swamps where water temperature up to 86°F (38°C) are the norm; others live in the icy lakes of Siberia and the Himalayas. Some of these monsters simply broadcast their eggs into the water, while others are mouthbrooders.

Both the kissing gourami and the gorami are reared for their flesh. Held in ponds constructed beneath swine pens, they feed on pig manure. The kissing gourami can reach a weight of about 2 lbs (1 kg); the gorami can exceed 17 lbs (7 kg). It is unusual to find specimens this large in a home aquarium, but beware when you see the label "giant gourami," which is often applied to this species, on a dealer's tank. While its inhabitants may be no more than 1.2 in (3 cm) long, they will very quickly grow to 12 in (30 cm) or more.

Some labyrinth fish, such as the climbing perches of the genus *Anabas*, move over the ground with the aid of spines located at the base of their gill covers and their pectoral fins, which serve them in lieu of feet.

Belontia species have not enjoyed the same degree of commercial success as the magnificent gouramis. Rarely offered for sale, they are kept only by hobbyists who specialize in this group of fish.

The several *Trichopsis* and *Parosphromenus* species are the smallest of the labyrinth fish. Shy and less vividly colored than the threadfin gouramis, they are found only in the tanks of the most dedicated enthusiasts. Some species make audible sounds when displaying to one another. The sound is created by the action of the muscles that move the pectoral fins, amplified by the labyrinth, which acts as a natural resonating chamber.

▲ *As its common name suggests, the Ceylon paradise fish is native to Sri Lanka. The fish shown here is a three-month-old juvenile.*

▲ The ocellated bushfish (Ctenopoma ocellatum) is rarely seen in captivity. Like the panther bushfish, it does not construct a bubble nest, but scatters its eggs freely.

▲ A remarkable characteristic of the spotted leaf fish (Polycentrus schomburgkii) is its ability to change color in a fraction of a second.

▶ The reproductive behavior of the chameleon perch (Badis badis) has elements in common with that of both labyrinth fish and cichlids.

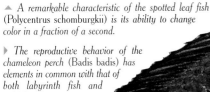

▲ Suitable only for the largest tanks, the gorami (Osphromenus gorami) constructs a nest 19 in (50 cm) in diameter and 10 in (25 cm) high.

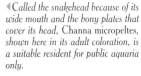

▲ Juvenile Channa micropeltes are extremely attractive fish. Do not be fooled—they are already formidable predators.

◀ Called the snakehead because of its wide mouth and the bony plates that cover its head, Channa micropeltes, shown here in its adult coloration, is a suitable resident for public aquaria only.

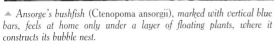

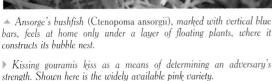

▲ Ansorge's bushfish (Ctenopoma ansorgii), marked with vertical blue bars, feels at home only under a layer of floating plants, where it constructs its bubble nest.

▶ Kissing gouramis kiss as a means of determining an adversary's strength. Shown here is the widely available pink variety.

▲ The chocolate gourami (Sphaerichthys osphromenoides) remains a delicate fish even after all of its maintenance requirements have been met.

▲ It is essential to house the croaking gourami (Trichopsis vittatus) in groups. They vocalize as they display to one another!

▲ A small fish for a small aquarium. The Anjungan licorice gourami (Parosphromenus ajunganensis).

Ornamental
Fish

▲ *The king of all tetras, the cardinal* (Paracheirodon axelrodi). *Although this species lives barely a year in nature, well-cared-for specimens can survive eight years or more in captivity.*

▶ *This silver-tip tetra* (Hemigrammus marginatus), *does not have an adipose fin. Some such individuals have been erroneously placed in the genus* Hasemania.

▲ *The glass bloodfin* (Prionobrama filigera) *closely resembles the true bloodfins of the genus* Aphyocharax *in body shape and coloration. An ideal beginner's fish.*

▲ *The flame tetra* (Hyphessobrycon flammeus), *or von Rio tetra, is hardy and easily bred. Now largely superceded by more colorful relatives, this species is seldom offered for sale.*

A Blind Fish

The sightless cave tetras of the Mexican tetra (Astyanax fasciatus) *have lost their black pigmentation and their fry hatch with sightless eyes that are overgrown with skin within two months. These fish were originally described as* Anoptichthys jordani, *but the presence of an intermediate tetra population of more or less pigmented fish—although with much smaller eyes and reduced visual acuity—demonstrates the error of that decision.*

Characoids:
New World Tetras

The characoid fishes, which number over a dozen families, include peaceful species as well as ferocious predators and scale eaters. They are native to Africa as well as both South and Central America. The true characins, also known to tropical fish fanciers as tetras, are the most widely known representatives of this group.

Tetras can be found in three different types of water, all characterized by very low concentrations of dissolved solids—thus very soft—which differ significantly in color and turbidity.

"White waters" are very turbid, with a dirty white or yellowish hue due to a heavy load of suspended solids. "Clear waters," or "green waters," are transparent but have a very faint yellow or green tint. The pH of white and clear water streams ranges from neutral to slightly acid, depending on the underlying geology of the river basin.

Finally, there are "black waters," perfectly transparent but very darkly tinted. Substances leached from decomposing vegetation turn these water bodies the color of strong tea and also often render them highly acidic.

Most tetras are schooling fish, typically to be found in running water. Active and powerful swimmers, most of these fish do not thrive when housed as solitary specimens and quickly show signs of stress in oxygen-poor waters. In addition to being well supplied with oxygen, their water must also be clean, soft, and slightly acid—filtering it through peat is advisable. The cover afforded by aquatic plants serves to set shy species at their ease.

Adults of all of these fish display some sexual dimorphism, although this may not always be obvious at first glance—males are more slender than females, more brightly colored, and have longer fins. Most characins are egg layers that scatter their eggs among fine-leafed aquatic plants, which provide a refuge for their newly hatched larvae and mobile fry.

▲ The red phantom tetra (Megalamphodus sweglesi) has two shortcomings as an aquarium resident: a short life span and sensitivity to high water temperatures.

▲ Although it usually swims with its head tilted upwards, this is not a sign that the hockey stick tetra (Thayeria boehlkei) is suffering from a lack of oxygen.

▲ The somber black coloration of Gymnocorymbus ternetzi has earned it the common name of black widow tetra. Better known as the black tetra, it seems to be a very merry widow indeed; individuals spend a lot of time displaying to one another.

▼ Through the agency of selective breeding, man has succeeded in creating this pink color form of Gymnocorymbus ternetzi. Would you believe a pink widow?

▲ The rummy-nose tetra (Hemigrammus bleheri), is routinely confused with two other similarly colored fishes, Hemigrammus rhodostomus and Petitella georgiae.

◀ The neon tetra (Paracheirodon innesi), sometimes known as the "little brother" of the cardinal, is often housed in community tanks whose excessively warm waters dull its colors and shorten its life span.

◀ The serpae tetra, represented here by the long-finned variety, is known to aquarists as either Hyphessobrycon serpae or H. callistus. Most commercially produced fish could be hybrids of these two species.

▲ Socolof's tetra (Hyphessobrycon socolofi) differs from the bleeding heart tetra (Hyphessobrycon erythrostigma) in the coloration of its dorsal and anal fins.

▼ The lemon tetra (Hyphessobrycon pulchripinnis) shows off its yellow coloration only when kept in soft water. Males have more intensely colored anal fins than females.

▲ The chaco tetra (Aphyocharax paraguayensis), while not brightly colored, adds contrast to a community aquarium.

◀ Aquarists are well acquainted with the emperor tetra (Nematobrycon palmeri), but the rainbow tetra (Nematobrycon lacortei), with its vivid red eyes, now has star billing.

Other Characins

▲ *The yellow congo tetra (Alestopetersius caudalis) is very similar in appearance to the Congo tetra. It is best not to house the two species together.*

▶ *The Congo tetra (Phenacogrammus interruptus), most popular of the African tetras. The dorsal and caudal fins of males develop long filaments.*

▲ *The African moon tetra (Bathyaethiops breuseghemi) is as yet unfamiliar to most aquarists. The red coloration on the back of this juvenile will intensify when it reaches adulthood.*

▼ *A timid fish, Nannaethiops unitaeniatus should be housed in a group to overcome its shyness.*

▼ *The stripped tigerfish (Hydrocynus vittatus), despite its formidable dentition, still plays second fiddle to its giant relative Hydrocynus goliath. H. goliath is even reputed to attack people and livestock.*

The Family Serrasalmidae comprises all those fish that have been erroneously called "piranhas." It is important to understand that this name has been bestowed on an assortment of very different fishes, all equated with the well-publicized flesh eater of the Amazon. Growing to a length of 8 to 10 in (20 to 25 cm), *Pygocentrus nattereri*, while indeed a carnivore, is much less ferocious than popularly portrayed, but there are other, plant-eating "piranhas" that, as juveniles, greatly resemble their carnivorous relative. Known to English-speaking aquarists as pacus, adults can exceed 2 ft (61 cm) in length and feed exclusively on fruits, seeds, and other vegetable foods in nature. Be prepared to act responsibly when buying any of the so-called "piranhas," be it a carnivore or herbivore. Thoughtless aquarists unable to manage their acquisitions are too quickly inclined to release them into the nearest body of water.

Hatchetfishes are noteworthy for their habit of escaping from predators by literally flying out of the water. The Family Gasteropelecidae includes the genera *Carnegiella*, *Gasteropelecus*, and *Thorocharax*.

Swimming head down, representatives of the genus *Anostomus* dwell in the shelter of submerged vegetation. They differ from their relatives of the genus *Leporinus* in their upturned mouths and prominent lips. It is amusing to watch the veritable gymnastic routine these fish must go through in order to feed.

The African tetras of the Family Alestidae tend to be more drably colored than their South American cousins. Only *Phenacogrammus interruptus* displays a comparable intensity of coloration. A schooling fish, it occupies the upper levels of the aquarium. The genus *Alestes* comprises several species that are imported as aquarium fish.

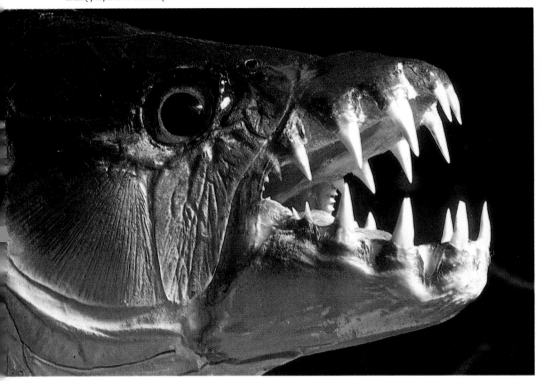

▲ *Ever on the alert for prey, the tubemouth pencilfish (Nannobrycon eques) swims head upwards. Thanks to its distinctively hinged jaws, it can swallow larger prey than one would expect given its diminutive size.*

▼ *Anostomus and Leporinus are from the Family Anostomidae. Their color pattern usually features stripes. An exception to this rule is the banded leporinus (Leporinus fasciatus).*

◀ The pectoral fins of hatchetfish are driven by powerful, highly modified muscles that make up 25 percent of the fish's body mass. Illustrated here is the silver hatchetfish (Gasteropelecus sternicla).

▼ Larger than its cousin the six-banded distichodus, the lussosso (Distichodus lussosso) reaches a length of 16 in (40 cm). A peaceful fish suitable for large—unplanted—tanks.

▶ A bad-tempered fish, but not as ferocious as the red-bellied piranha, the bucktooth tetra (Exodon paradoxus) is not recommended for novice fish keepers.

▼ Native to the Congo River and to date seldom imported, Pheracogrammus altus has proven rather delicate in captivity. Careful attention to water quality and housing the fish in groups are important.

▼ The splash tetra (Copella cf. arnoldi) lays its eggs out of water on the underside of an overhanging leaf. The male then has the essential task of keeping them moist by splashing them with water.

▲ A herbivore, the six-banded distichodus (Distichodus sexfasciatus) must be fed lettuce and spinach, but even this will not prevent it from eating aquatic plants. Such large fish as this are rarely to be found in hobbyists' aquaria.

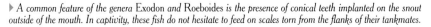

▲ This young red-bellied piranha (Pygocentrus nattereri) will lose its spotted color pattern as it matures.

▶ A common feature of the genera Exodon and Roeboides is the presence of conical teeth implanted on the snout outside of the mouth. In captivity, these fish do not hesitate to feed on scales torn from the flanks of their tankmates.

Cypriniform Fishes: The Barbs

The cyprinoform fish comprise only five families, three of them well known to tropical fish fanciers: Cyprinidae (carps and minnows), Cobitidae (true loaches), and Gyrinocheilidae (Asian algae eaters). Since the recent importation of the so-called Asian plecos, *Gasteromyzon* and *Neogasteromyzon* spp. and the Chinese sailfin shark, *Myxocyprinus asiaticus*, the Families Balitoridae (hillstream loaches) and Catostomidae (suckers) have been added to this roster. Cyprinoform fish are to be found in all of the earth's fresh waters, either as native residents or as exotic species successfully naturalized as food fish, as exemplified by the carp.

The smallest known cypriniform fish is slightly over ½ in (1 cm) long; the largest recorded specimen of *Barbus tor*, caught at the end of the nineteenth century, measured 10 ft (3 m) in length. As for their anatomy, cypriniform fish lack jaw teeth but do have very well-developed pharyngeal dentition. Although a few species do enter brackish water, they are essentially freshwater fish. About 80 percent of cypriniform fishes are members of the Family Cyprinidae.

Barbs are lively, colorful egg-laying fish. They derive their name from the fine barbels on either side of the mouth. It is best not to house barbs with more placid fish species. As long as they are given a varied diet that includes some live foods, and clean water, their aquarium husbandry poses no problems. They have a tendency to nibble soft-leafed plants.

Several years ago, barbs were split into several genera (*Barbus*, *Barbodes*, *Capoeta*, and *Puntius*), based upon the number of pairs of oral barbels a given species possesses. Today there is controversy over this system of classification. All the species discussed here are placed in the genus *Barbus*.

▲ *The striped barb, (Barbus eugrammus) is sometimes sold as* Barbus lineatus, *a different species. The former possesses a single pair of oral barbels; the latter does not.*

▼ *Be aware when purchasing small T-barbs (Barbus lateristriga) that adults grow over 6 in (15 cm) long.*

▲ *The black ruby (Barbus nigrofasciatus). The head and front half of the body of displaying males become bright red.*

▲ *A gentle fish characterized by neither the swiftness nor the bad manners of some of its relatives, the cherry barb (Barbus titteya) does not eat the new growth of aquatic plants.*

▲ *You will also encounter the ember barb (Barbus fasciatus) under the name* Barbus megalampyx, *a synonym. A strong swimmer, it requires a large tank.*

◀ *The tiger barb (Barbus tetrazona) is all too often housed in a community aquarium with such long-finned species as angelfish and guppies. Badly nipped fins are the sad fate of their tankmates.*

▲ Under ideal conditions, the golden dwarf barb (Barbus gelius) sports an ebony and gold color pattern. It measures only 1 in (2.5 cm) when adult.

▲ Despite its bright coloration, the gold barb, or Barbus schuberti, is seldom offered for sale. It is actually a golden type of Barbus semifasciolatus.

◀ The velvet body of the green variety of the Sumatra barb.

▲ The quiet five-banded barb (Barbus pentazona) has been split into several subspecies, based on the size and shape of its lateral bars.

▶ The rosy barb (Barbus conchonius) does not require a heated tank. Some selectively bred forms have an intense pink coloration, others have long, flowing fins.

▲ The Odessa barb was developed in Moscow from Barbus ticto. Note the velvety sheen on the flanks of the green color form of the tiger barb.

▲ Two male Barbus bandulla, the dominant individual below. The subordinate male, above, has assumed female coloration to escape his attentions.

▲ The black spot on its caudal peduncle has earned Barbus filamentosus its name of blackspot barb, the only element of the juvenile pattern of black markings that persists into adulthood.

◀ The ghost barb, an artificially selected color form of the tiger barb.

Cypriniform Fishes: Danios, Rasboras, and Their Relatives

▲ *The pygmy rasbora* (Rasbora maculata) *is not only the smallest of the rasoras, but at 1 in (2.5 cm) long, it is among the smallest known cyprinids.*

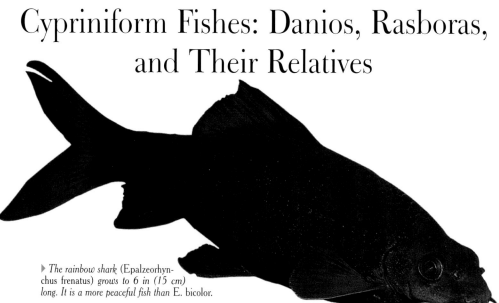

▶ *The rainbow shark* (Epalzeorhynchus frenatus) *grows to 6 in (15 cm) long. It is a more peaceful fish than* E. bicolor.

▲ *The harlequin* (Rasbora heteromorpha), *the most widely sold rasbora, spawns in an upside-down position.*

Danios were fist bred by amateur aquarists at the beginning of the twentieth century. At that time, aquariums were not heated, so hobbyists could keep only fish able to withstand low water temperatures. The danios were waiting in the wings and the zebra danio became a real star.

Hardy and easily bred, danios remain very popular. Native to India and Southeast Asia, they typically school in creeks and brooks, although some species also inhabit still waters. Females can be easily recognized by their rounder bellies. Danios shed their eggs in midwater and the successful rearing of their fry requires a supply of microscopic food scaled to the size of their mouths.

Rasboras are likewise small fishes, whose coloration ranges from cherry red to drab gray, depending on the species in question. They live in schools in the soft waters of Southeast Asia.

Cousins of the danios and rasboras, the so-called black sharks of the genus *Epalzeorhynchus* are also native to this region. Bottom grubbers and, in some instances, algae grazers, they are often rather quarrelsome fish that grow too large to live comfortably in most home aquariums. The red-tailed black shark *(Epalzeorhynchus bicolor)* is nevertheless popular with tropical fish fanciers. It is bred commercially in Thailand. An injection of hormones derived from the pituitary of the common carp triggers egg laying a few hours later. This technique, used only by professional breeders, is as effective as it is draconian.

▲ *A school of giant scissortail rasboras* (Rasbora caudimaculata) *in a well-planted tank is a magnificent sight. This fish grows over 4 in (10 cm) long.*

◀ Tanichthys linni *is closely related to the white cloud,* Tanichthys albonubes, *from which it differs in the color of its fins. Shown here are specimens of a long-finned variety, known as the meteor minnow.*

A Naked Minnow

Still rare—and expensive— Sawbwa resplendens is a magnificent fish. Unfortunately, the female lacks the male's red snout and caudal fin lobes. Its common name of naked rasbora is warranted by its scaleless body.

▲ *This blue form of the harlequin is a naturally occurring mutant.*

▼ *The red-tailed black shark* (Epalzeorhynchus bicolor) *likes to graze algae from an aquarium's decor. It becomes more aggressive as it grows older.*

▲ *The pearl danio, (Brachydanio albolineatus), dull gray in dealers' tanks, turns into the most beautiful of all danios after settling into its new home.*

▶ *One sometimes finds "contaminants" such as this lemon-yellow* Rasbora daniconius *in shipments of rasboras from Thailand.*

▼ *A well-planted backdrop is essential to show the red-railed rasbora* (Rasbora borapetensis) *to best advantage.*

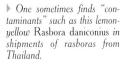

▲ *The zebra danio* (Brachydanio rerio) *has become a virtual guinea pig for genetic research because of its rapid growth and the ease with which it can be bred.*

▲ Danio regina, *at 5 in (13 cm) when adults, grows larger than the giant danio* (Danio aequipinnatus).

▲ *It is unclear whether the leopard danio* (Brachydanio frankei) *is a hybrid or an artificially selected color variety of* Brachydanio rerio.

▲ *The false harlequin* (Rasbora espei) *is smaller and redder than* Rasbora heteromorpha.

▲ *The scales of Pangio kuhli are visible beneath its skin.*

▶ *The only Asian member of the Family Catostomidae has recently made its aquarium debut. The Chinese sailfin sucker (*Myxocyprinus asiaticus*) can grow to 16 to 20 in (40 to 80 cm) in nature.*

▲ *Its strikingly contrasted color pattern assures Botia cf. histrionica a promising future in the tanks of loach fanciers.*

▼ *Despite its flattened form and bottom-hugging posture, Neogasteromyzon cheni is not a loricariid catfish but rather a hillstream loach of the Family Balitoridae.*

Cypriniform Fishes: Loaches and Oddballs

Scales covered by a layer of skin are the most distinctive characteristic of the loaches. Several pairs of oral barbels and an elongate, even snakelike body are other defining features. These "naked" fishes are extremely sensitive to dissolved chemicals; copper-based medicines can prove lethal to them.

Loaches as popularly understood comprise about 100 species in two families, the Cobitidae (true loaches) and the Balitoridae (hillstream loaches). The species of aquaristic interest are almost all native to India and Southeast Asia. They use their oral barbels to dislodge worms and insect larvae from the bottom, their main preoccupation. Loaches are armed with two strong cephalic spines, usually carried just below the eye, which they erect when displaying aggressively or fighting.

The clown loach (*Botia macracartha*) is the best known of the group. It can grow to 8 in (20 cm) in captivity and easily double that length in nature. Its exact life expectancy, which

appears to be several decades, is not known for sure. The only superficially obvious difference between the sexes is the female's rounder belly. At dusk, it is not unusual for a pair of clown loaches to nestle down side by side and spend the entire night in such intimacy.

Diminutive and snakelike, kuhli loaches occur throughout Southeast Asia and the principal islands of Indonesia. They reach a maximum size of 4 in (10 cm). Essentially nocturnal fish, they come out only at dusk, but they can be induced to leave their hiding places earlier than usual by feeding them at a predictable time. As they are schooling fish, it is advisable to house each species in groups of at least five specimens. Kuhli loaches seldom spawn in captivity, but successful breeding was observed in Europe in 1975.

▶ *The oral barbels typical of cyprinids are clearly visible in this photo of* Luciosoma setigerum. *Adults can measure 10 in (25 cm) long.*

▲ The zebra loach (Botia striata) is an elegant species of the genus.

▶ A number of recently imported loach species, such as this Botia cf. geto, have very similar color patterns and are thus not easily identified.

▲ The female reticulated loach (Botia lohachata) can grow to 4 in (10 cm) in captivity. Males remain much smaller. This ripe female deposited her eggs in a pit dug in the gravel several days after this photo was taken.

▲ The uniform flesh-toned base color and black dorsal stripe of the skunk loach (Botia morleti) set it apart from all known loaches. It is usually sold under the name Botia horae.

◀ The bala shark (Balantiocheilus melanopterus) is a peaceful fish that must be kept in groups. It can grow to 14 in (35 cm) long.

▼ The clown loach (Botia macracantha) can produce clearly audible clicking sounds. This behavior, accompanied by the erection of its subocular spines, is a feature of aggressive displays.

The Dwarf Loach

A reportedly endangered species, the dwarf loach (Botia sidthimunki) vanished from the trade for many years. As with the great majority of loaches, aquarists were dependent upon wild-caught specimens of this species. It is now bred, although infrequently, in Asia.

▲ The broad central and pectoral fins of this hillstream loach (Gasteromyzon cf. borneensis) act as suction cups that allow it to hold its position in the face of the strongest currents.

◀ There are two subspecies of the kuhli loach (Pangio kuhli). They differ in the shape of the bars that adorn their flanks.

Live-bearers True and False: The Genus *Poecilia* and Its Relatives

▲ *Native to Haiti, the ornate limia (Limia ornata) has the annoying habit of cannibalizing its newborn fry.*

▼ *A young male red double swordtail show guppy. The fins of this youngster are not yet fully developed.*

W hy make a distinction between true and false live-bearers? The confusion of these two reproductive modalities is easily understandable when an aquarist observes a female guppy deliver her brood of young. Newborn fry are, after a few moments of torpor, fully mobile and can begin feeding almost immediately, although they must quickly take shelter from potential predators. Less evident is what has gone on inside of the female before the moment of birth. Clearly, the first step in this process was her insemination by a male. He accomplishes this feat through the agency of his anal fin, which has been transformed into a copulatory organ, the gonopodium. Females are capable of storing male sperm, so a single insemination can fertilize more than one clutch of eggs and thus give rise to several subsequent broods of young. The fertilized eggs develop within the female's body. When they hatch, she immediately gives birth to the resulting fry. This process is known as *ovoviviparity* and those fish that practice it fully warrant the designation "false live-bearer." All the representatives of the Families Poeciliidae and Anablepidae are ovoviviparous. Both true and false live-bearers are far less prolific than are egg layers of a comparable size. Their smaller broods contain far fewer but much larger young than do those of egg layers and have a much better likelihood of surviving the hazards of childhood because of their larger size. This allows them to bypass the extremely vulnerable larval stage to which most egg-laying fish are irrevocably bound.

The live-bearing fishes of the Family Poeciliidae are the best known of all warm-water aquarium fish. They are easily kept and bred, with vibrant coloration. The guppy (*Poecilia reticulata*) hails from the island of Trinidad and coastal rivers of northern Venezuela. Commercial breeders in Singapore and Malaysia have succeeded in producing an unprecedented range of artificially selected varieties that differ from their wild ancestors in both color and fin development.

▲ *The male green sailfin molly (Poecilia latipinna) has an enormous dorsal fin that he spreads to its fullest extent during courtship.*

▼ *Male wild guppy from Guyana. These fish are not selectively bred to preserve their genetic heritage.*

▲ *The pedigree of the various strains of highly colored mollies is not immediately obvious. As a rule, these color forms are the result of controlled hybridization between* Poecilia velifera *and* Poecilia latipinna.

▸ *The male repeatedly sniffs at the female's vent to determine if she is ready for mating.*

▲ A male electric blue veiltail guppy, developed by a dedicated guppy fancier with the show circuit in mind.

▼ Three male red veiltail guppies of the aquarium trade.

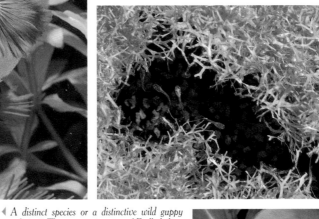

▲ A male of the widely available panther veiltail guppy. Fish with this pattern of black pigment are also offered for sale as snakeskin guppies.

◄ Day-old guppy fry photographed in a small aquarium with floating plants.

▼ A female golden guppy paired with a red leopard veiltail male. What color patterns will result from this union of two selected guppy varieties?

◄ A distinct species or a distinctive wild guppy population? The taxonomic status of Endler's live-bearer (Poecilia sp.) is unclear, but its resistance to selective breeding programs is a fact.

▼ In pursuit of further novelty, breeders work with mutations whose effects are clearly deleterious. Do grotesque forms as these balloon mollies need to be produced? The future of this strain is uncertain. Most fry die within a few days of birth; the survivors are weak and stunted.

▲ A male Endler's guppy inseminating a female with his gonopodium.

▲ A nondescript little fish, the yellow girardinus (Girardinus metallicus) is appreciated only by live-bearer specialists. The length of the male's gonopodium is impressive.

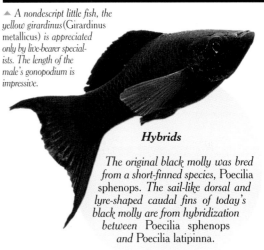

Hybrids

The original black molly was bred from a short-finned species, Poecilia sphenops. The sail-like dorsal and lyre-shaped caudal fins of today's black molly are from hybridization between Poecilia sphenops and Poecilia latipinna.

Swordtails, Platies, and Some True Live-bearers

▲ Native to the highlands of Mexico, goodeids do not tolerate elevated water temperatures. Shown here a male Ilyodon xantusi, a species rarely available commercially.

▶ A tank with several varieties of a single species (Xiphophorus maculatus) makes for a tasteful display. A mixture of many different species is best avoided in smaller tanks.

▲ A male northern mountain swordtail (Xiphophorus nezahualcoyotl). Few aquarists have had the opportunity to acquire this magnificent rarity.

▲ Hobbyists have made the red swordtail the most popular color form of X. helleri. The male can be easily recognized by his gonopodium and the swordlike extension of his tail.

The commercial production of platies and swordtails is also a specialty of Asian breeders. Starting with olive-gray, green-, and red-striped wild swordtails, their efforts have given rise to the numerous aquarium strains of *Xiphophorus helleri*. One can now buy swordtails with veil-like fins in a wide selection of velvety, saturated colors.

House swordtails (*Xiphophorus helleri*) and platies (*Xiphophorus maculatus* and *X. variatus*) in a well-planted tank, whose aquascaping will provide shelter to both adults and fry, and take care that their water is clean and well circulated. In nature, these fish selectively graze algal mats in search of small invertebrates. This can also be observed in captivity. They should have a varied diet, supplemented by occasional feedings of mosquito larvae, their favorite food. The use of a breeding trap to confine gravid females is highly stressful. It is far safer to move the expectant mother into a small, heavily planted and well-aerated tank of her own to give birth.

True live-bearing fish nourish their developing embryos by means of placenta-like structures that link their circulatory systems with that of the mother. The practitioners of this reproductive pattern are the highland live-bearers (Family Goodeidae), halfbeaks (Family Hemiramphidae), and freshwater stingrays (Family Potamoryonidae), whose pelvic fins have been transformed into paired copulatory organs, the claspers. Because of their large adult size, which dictates housing them in very large tanks, and the prices they command, they are beyond the reach of most beginning hobbyists.

As for halfbeaks, the Family Hemiramphidae is poorly represented in fresh waters. Most halfbeaks live in either brackish waters or in the ocean.

▲ This freshwater stingray (Potamotrygon hystrix) is not a fish for everyone. The 2-in-long (4 cm) barbed spines implanted in its whiplike tail can inflict painful wounds.

◀ Depending upon the angle and intensity of the light striking its body, the color of this platy can shift from sky to midnight blue. This is a recently developed color variety.

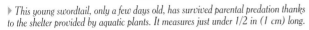

Tail First

This female Xenotoca eiseni is about to give birth. The fry are fully developed and have begun to move around inside their mother's body. At birth, they retain traces of the trophotaeniae, a threadlike structure analogous to the umbilical cord of mammals. As long as their tank is heavily planted and their parents well fed, the fry have a good chance of surviving parental cannibalism during their first hours of life. With the passage of time, this risk diminishes substantially.

▶ This young swordtail, only a few days old, has survived parental predation thanks to the shelter provided by aquatic plants. It measures just under 1/2 in (1 cm) long.

▼ This well-rounded female red swordtail will shortly deliver her young.

▲ This wild male swordtail's coloration is more subtle than that of selectively bred varieties of X. helleri.

▼ The variatus platy (Xiphophorus variatus) takes second place to X. maculatus in the number of selectively bred varieties it offers to aquarists, but this highfin form has been successful.

▼ Hardy and available in a wide range of colors, the platy (Xiphophorus maculatus) is a particular favorite of novice fish fanciers.

▲ The stocky body of this male Xenotoca eiseni is testimony to his virility. First few rays of his anal fin are modified to serve as a copulatory organ.

◀ These platies are the result of controlled crosses between X. variatus and X. maculatus.

▲ The halfbeaks of the Family Hemiramphidae are surface-dwelling fishes that prey on stranded terrestrial insects. Shown here is a male Nomoramphus liemi, easily recognizable by the fleshy projection on his chin.

Killifish

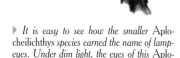

▲ *These are three known male color forms of* Nothobranchius eggersi: *red, blue, and, shown here, red and blue.*

▶ *Male dusky pearlfish (Cynolebias nigripinnis) are quite aggressive even though they reach a length of barely 2 in (4 cm).*

Killifish derive their name from *kil*, the Dutch word for creek or brook. The Dutch settlers of New York first coined this name for *Fundulus heteroclitus*, and "killifish" has since come to be applied to other fish of the Family Cyprinodontidae. Killifish can be found on every continent except Australia. Approximately 450 species are presently recognized. Most species grow to between 2 and 3 in (5 to 7 cm) long, although a number of *Aplocheilichthys* species barely reach 1 inch (2.5 cm) in length, while the giants of the group, representatives of the Andean genus *Orestias*, approach 12 in (30 cm). For the most part, killifish feed upon stranded terrestrial insects. They thus often live in prox-imity to stands of floating plants, while their eyes and mouths are well adapted for taking prey from the water's surface.

As each species exists as a complex of discrete populations, each restricted to a particular body of water and characterized by a distinctive color pattern, a more precise system of classification is essential. It is thus normal for the name of its collecting site to be attached to the scientific name of a given species, minimizing the risk of accidental hybridization between discrete populations, and thus serving to safeguard their genetic integrity.

There are two broad categories of killifish: annual species and perennial species. Annual killies live less than a year. Like butterflies, they hatch, grow to maturity, and breed within a few months. These fish inhabit seasonally flooded marshes that disappear during the dry season. They deposit their eggs in the soil. These "resting eggs" undergo a *diapause*, or period of arrested development that allows them to remain dormant until the arrival of the next rainy season triggers hatching. This life history characteristic makes it possible for killifish enthusiasts to successfully exchange fertile eggs packed in barely damp peat by mail. Perennial killifish are found in permanent bodies of water. As their name implies, these fish can live for several years. They deposit their eggs, which do not undergo a prolonged resting period, among the leaves and roots of aquatic plants.

▶ *It is easy to see how the smaller Aplocheilichthys species earned the name of lampeyes. Under dim light, the eyes of this Aplocheilichthys normani seem to glow in the dark.*

▼ *A diminutive marvel from the wilds of Brazil,* Cynolebias fulminatus *is an annual killifish whose eggs take five months to hatch.*

▲ *Despite its aggressive temperament, the blue gularis (Aphyosemion sjoestedti) is one of the most popular killifish species. It can grow to over 4 in (10 cm) in length.*

▼ Aphyosemion walkeri *can be easily recognized by its dusky shoulder spot.*

◀ This selectively bred color variety of the lineatus panchax (Aplocheilus lineatus), or the golden lineatus, lacks the distinctive pattern of fine dark lines on the flanks of this species. The ripe female can be recognized by her more rounded ventral region.

▶ Fertile eggs of A. lineatus as they appear three hours post-spawning. Long, sticky filaments attach them firmly to the leaves and stems of aquatic plants.

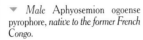

▼ Male Aphyosemion ogoense pyrophore, native to the former French Congo.

▲ Aquarists tend to overlook the Florida flagfish (Jordanella floridae). This species is the only killifish in which the male actively tends his clutch of eggs.

▼ The only species of its genus, the Tanganyikan giant lampeye (Lamprichthys tanganicanus) deposits its eggs in crevices in the rocks.

▲ The Aphyosemion australe was one of the first killifish to be successfully bred by European aquarists. Here a male of the artificially selected orange color form spreads his splendid fins.

▲ There are three known natural populations of the clown killifish (Pseudepiplatys annulatus). Unfortunately, all three were hybridized in captivity. This diminutive fish barely reaches 1½ in (3.5 to 4 cm) in total length. It is rather fragile and successfully bred only by experienced killifish fanciers.

▲ Not as well known as many other types of killifish, the giant lampeyes of the genus Procatopus have a reputation—not always deserved—for fragility. The pair of Procatropus aberrans shown here is about to spawn. The female will deposit her eggs in the accessible crannies of this porous rock.

◀ The eggs of Procatopus aberrans take a long time to hatch; 15 days post-spawning, these well-developed embryos have begun to move around within the confines of the chorionic membrane.

Rainbowfish

The fish of the Order Atheriniformes are found in marine and freshwater habitats in both the temperate zone and the tropics. As their name suggests, the Australasian rainbowfish are native to the fresh waters of northern Australia and New Guinea. The Family Melanotaeniidae comprises six genera and about sixty described species. The number continues to increase steadily as new species are constantly being discovered. One of these new discoveries is *Melanotaenia praecox*, a diminutive rainbowfish that barely reaches 2 in (5 cm) in length. Most other representatives of the family grow somewhat larger, ranging from 3¾ to 6 in (12 to 15 cm) long. The bodies of Australasian rainbowfish become very deep as they grow older, while their heads remain relatively small in size. In nature, these fish are typically found in the well-planted shallows of lakes, often in large schools. They mostly feed on stranded terrestrial insects, which they take from the water's surface.

These fish are easily bred. Spawning occurs early in the morning, preferably in those portions of the aquarium illuminated by natural sunlight. Females lay several eggs each day. The eggs are deposited in aquatic plants, to which they adhere by means of a long filament.

Madagascar is home to the closely related Family Bedotiidae, which comprises three described and five undescribed species. *Bedotia madagascariensis* is the only species commercially available.

▲ *This seven-day-old* Glossolepis incisus *egg will shortly hatch.*

▼ *A dull gray fish in a retailer's tanks, the Lake Kutubu blue rainbowfish (*Melanotaenia lacustris*) offers prospective purchasers few hints of its true beauty.*

▲ *A courting male Bleher's rainbowfish (*Chilatherina bleheri*). Among male melanotaeniids, a luminous yellow or blue-white forehead stripe is indicative of sexual activity.*

▼ *These* Melanotaenia praecox *eggs have been deposited on fine-leafed aquatic plants, to which they adhere by means of threadlike filaments. Females produce several eggs daily over the course of each period of reproductive activity.*

▲ *This is the diminutive newcomer that popularized aquarium rainbowfish.* Melanotaenia praecox *is a dwarf species that seldom grows more than 2 in (4 to 5 cm) long under aquarium conditions.*

▼ *A close-up view of the scales of the yellow rainbowfish (*Melanotaenia herbertaxelrodi*).*

▲ When kept in groups, males of the yellow rainbowfish (Melanotaenia herbertaxelrodi) establish a clear dominance hierarchy.

▲ As many recognized subspecies of Melanotaenia splendida are very similar in appearance, reliable data on its point of origin are essential.

▶ Bedotia madagascariensis is found in the hills of the east central coast of Madagascar. The caudal fin of most males is edged in red, that of females in iridescent white.

▲ Boeseman's rainbowfish (Melanotaenia boesemani) launched the current wave of interest in Australasian rainbowfish. Large and active, it requires a spacious aquarium to prosper.

▼ The elegant Pseudomugil furcatus is a representative of the related Australasian Family Pseudomugilidae. Beautiful but rare (and consequently high-priced), this species is not easy to maintain in captivity.

◀ Irian Jaya, the Indonesian portion of the island of New Guinea, conceals many aquaristic treasures. Notable among them is the threadfin rainbowfish (Iriatherina werneri). Females lack the long filaments that adorn the dorsal and anal fins of males.

▶ Although it is found in only a very restricted area in northern New Guinea, the red rainbowfish (Glossolepis incisus) quickly won a secure place among aquarium fish. If housed in a large aquarium, it will spawn even in a community tank.

▲ The body shape of juvenile Australasian rainbowfish is quite ordinary. It is only after several years of growth that they develop the deep bodies so characteristic of the family. Shown here is a young male Melanotaenia trifasciata.

◀ Breeders have produced a number of rainbowfish hybrids. These fish may be a Melanotaenia splendida and Melanotaenia boesemani crossing.

An Assortment of Oddballs

▲ *The male black arrowana (Osteoglossum ferreirai) is a mouthbrooder, carrying his brood until the young become mobile, at a length of 3¼ to 4 in (8 to 10 cm). Its juvenile color pattern of yellow stripes on a dark brown to black background has earned it its common name.*

▶ *Under polarized light, this scale of Scleropages jardini reveals the distinct pattern of rings that mark the growth history of this specimen.*

▲ *This yolk sac of this young common arrowana (Osteoglossum bicirrhosum), newly released by his father, has not been entirely absorbed. Adults grow to 4 ft (1.2 m) in length.*

Members of the Order Osteoglossiformes are notable for their retention of a number of primitive characteristics. These are for the most part very large fish, as exemplified by *Arapaima gigas.* Capable of attaining lengths in excess of 8 ft (2.5 m), it is one of the largest known freshwater fish. Amateur fish keepers and public aquariums often display its "smaller" relatives of the genera *Osteoglossum* and *Scleropages.* The order also includes the Old World knifefish of the Family Notopteridae. The genera *Notopterus* and *Xenomystus* are most familiar to hobbyists. These fish move through the water by undulating their long anal fins. The superficially similar South American knifefish, which include the genera *Eigenmannia* and *Sternopygus,* are representatives of the Order Gymnotiformes. They are most closely related to the characin-like fishes.

With approximately 200 species restricted to the fresh waters of Africa, the Family Mormyridae is by far the largest of the order. These fish not only generate an electric field but are capable of sending, receiving, and analyzing electrical signals. This ability allows these fish to not only navigate the turbid waters of their African homes, but to locate prey and communicate with conspecifics and even with other species of "electric" fish. The wavelength of their electrical output varies between species, while conspecifics can communicate with one another by varying its frequency. The so-called elephant-nosed fish of the genera *Gnathonemus* and *Campylomormyrus,* and the "baby whales" of the genera *Marcusenius* and *Pollimyrus* are the most commonly available representatives of the group.

The puffers, representatives of the Order Tetraodontiformes, are well represented in the marine realm. The notorious fugu, beloved of Japanese gourmets, is a marine puffer. Only a few freshwater puffers have attracted the interest of aquarists. They are notable for their unusual dentition, in which the teeth in both upper and lower jaws have fused together to form a veritable beak.

There are other kinds of unusual fish to be found in the tanks of hobbyists with a taste for the bizarre; however, but most are seldom offered for sale.

▲ *The behavior of the peacock gudgeon (Tateurndina ocellicauda) resembles in many respects that of a diminutive cichlid. Here a male guards his clutch of eggs, deposited within a bamboo stalk. Although these eggs are only 48 hours old, the embryos possess well-developed eyes.*

◀ *Two of the eleven known Polypterus species: the uniformly gray-brown Senegal bichir (Polyperus senegalus) and the Congo bichir (Polypterus delhezi). All bichirs have an elongated body and many small independent dorsal fins, or pinnules.*

◀ The Congo puffer (Tetraodon mbu), a fish capable of attaining a length of just under 3 ft (80 cm) in nature, obviously must be housed in a spacious tank.

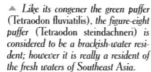

▲ Like its congener the green puffer (Tetraodon fluviatilis), the figure-eight puffer (Tetraodon steindachneri) is considered to be a brackish-water resident; however it is really a resident of the fresh waters of Southeast Asia.

Elephant Fish

The fleshy process on the chin of the elephant-nosed mormyrid (Gnathonemus petersii) allows it to rummage through the detritus carpeting the bottom of its native rivers and detect its prey, the aquatic insects concealed therein. The brain of this species is particularly well developed.

▲ The ghost knifefish (Sternpygus sp.) can grow over 1 yd (1 m) long in nature, large enough to be exploited as a food fish. In captivity they become tame and take food from their keeper's fingers.

▲ As its name suggests, the African lungfish (Protopterus annectens) does possess a functioning lung. Thanks to this organ, it can survive the dry season buried in a cocoon of mud. Its unusually developed paired fins allow it to "walk" over the bottom.

▶ Despite its attractively contrasted color pattern, the fire eel (Mastacembelus erythrotaenia) is a voracious nocturnal predator.

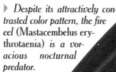

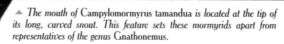

▲ The mouth of Campylomormyrus tamandua is located at the tip of its long, curved snout. This feature sets these mormyrids apart from representatives of the genus Gnathonemus.

▼ With its blue eyes, the Nile puffer (Tetraodon fahaka) is a charmer, but it grows over 8 in (20 cm) long and is an incorrigible "nipper."

▲ The African butterfly fish (Pantodon buchholzi) is another primitive osteoglossiform fish. It is capable of making prodigious leaps out of the water in pursuit of its insect prey.

Whiskers
and Armor

Corydoras

▲ *The color pattern of* Corydoras bolivianus *is very similar to that of the emerald brochis (Brochis splendens), but can easily be recognized by its shorter-based dorsal fin.*

▼ Corydoras trilineatus *is usually sold under the name* Corydoras julii, *a valid but much less frequently seen species.*

C atfish, as their name suggests, have mouths surrounded by one or more pairs of barbels, or whiskers, which permit them to detect prey as they rummage. Catfish lack true scales, although the flanks of some species are adorned with a series of bony plaques. In some families, these plates enclose the fish in a veritable strongbox, its armor. Others, the so-called "naked" catfish, are lacking such protection.

Catfish can be found on every continent except Antarctica, typically in fresh water, although some brackish water species are known. Catfish are divided among 31 families. Roughly 400 genera and some 2,200 species of catfish are currently recognized, but the total number keeps increasing as more discoveries result in the description of new taxa. In size, catfish range from the diminutive *Corydoras pygmaeus*, which barely measures 1 in (2.5 cm) in length, through *Pangasianodon gigas*, terror of fishermen on the Mekong River, whose stocky body can measure over 9 ft (2.7 m) long.

Corydoras are armored catfish, representatives of the Family Callichthyidae, which comprises seven genera. Thanks to analyses of their DNA, their relationships are relatively well known. Because they are thought of as the "clean-up squad," *Corydoras* are often inadequately fed in the home aquarium. Forced to make do with leftovers and to adapt to whatever water conditions prevail in a community aquarium, it is no surprise that these catfish are usually disinclined to breed in captivity. However, if individuals of the same species are housed in groups and well fed, *Corydoras* are quite willing to display their remarkable breeding behavior, but the fact remains that the fry of a number of species are rather delicate and not easily reared. Fifteen years ago aquarists were able to obtain any species except *Corydoras aeneus, C. julii,* and *C. paleatus.* Today, importers' price lists regularly offer 50 of the 140 described species of the genus.

Corydoras are from South America, the great majority of species native to the Amazon basin. They prefer to live in clear, well-oxygenated water, and are very much at home in flowing streams, where they move about in schools hundreds—sometime thousands—strong. Depending upon their point of origin, *Corydoras* can withstand temperatures as low as 50°F (10°C) and as high as 90°F (32°C). These catfish have two features that aquarists would be well advised to note. First, they respond to oxygen-poor surroundings by gulping air at the water's surface, so the cover of their aquarium must never be flush with the surface of the water, or they can suffocate. Second, their dorsal and pectoral fins have strong spines, so they must be handled with care.

▲ Corydoras guapore *is rare, and thus quite expensive.*

▼ *Unusual behavior for a* Corydoras. *This* Corydoras polystictus *is keeping an eye on developments at the bottom of the tank from his perch in the plants.*

◄ *A school of young bronze corys.* Corydoras aeneus *is the most easily bred species of the genus. Spawns range from 200 to 300 eggs.*

The Family Callichthyidae

The Family Callichthyidae comprises seven genera. Aspidoras, Brochis, which can be distinguished from Corydoras by the greater number of rays in the dorsal fin (top right photo), and Corydoras, the best-known genus of the lot, comprise one group of superficially similar species. The second group consists of the genera Callichthys, Cataphractops, Dianema (bottom right photo), and Hoplosternum.

▶A recent import, Corydoras cf. adolfoi is more intensely colored than the true bearer of that name.

▼ Corydoras barbatus is one of the most attractive and largest known species of the genus. A high-altitude resident, it cannot long tolerate temperatures in excess of 72°F (22°C). Its ideal temperature range is 65 to 70°F (18 to 20°C).

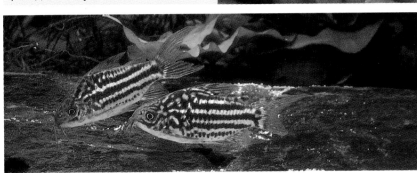

▲ The pattern of sexual dimorphism typical of Corydoras is evident in this pair of Corydoras napoensis. The female (lower fish) has a stockier build and more rounded ventral profile than the male.

◀ The peppered cory (Corydoras paleatus) made its debut in 1880. It is so easily bred that it is tied with Corydoras aeneus for first place in overall availability.

▼ Corydoras panda, whose pale beige body with its contrasting black markings is somewhat reminiscent of the giant panda, was an absolute sensation a few years ago.

▲ Corydoras davidsandsi deposits its eggs at random on any available solid surface: the sides of its aquarium, rocks, or, as can be seen in this photo, the underside of an Anubias leaf. These eggs are 20 hours old.

▲ The first, spiny ray of the dorsal fin is clearly visible in this Corydoras araguaiaensis. Corydoras can lock their dorsal and pectoral spines in place, a mechanism that affords them a defense when attacked by predators.

▲ This young Corydoras metae, barely 1 in (3 cm) long, is a miniature version of its parents, perfect in every detail.

▲ Adult Corydoras hastatus attain a length of barely 1 in (3 cm), making it one of the real dwarfs of the genus.

▲ *Ancistrus temminckii is perhaps the easiest catfish to breed in captivity. The dorsal and caudal of juveniles (the individual shown here is four months old) sport iridescent white margins that grow progressively smaller and ultimately disappear as they grow older.*

▲ *This ventral view of a typical "pleco" clearly shows the thick lips, ornamented with fleshy papillae and the two bands of fine teeth present in each jaw.*

▶ *The recently discovered zebra pleco (Hypancistrus zebra) is a jewel every aquarist yearns to own. Unfortunately, the price of wild-caught specimens is prohibitive and techniques for breeding it on a commercial scale have yet to be developed.*

▼ *Otocinclus flexilis can grow to 2 in (7 cm) long.*

Plecos and Their Relatives

The current infatuation with the Family Callichthyidae has given rise to great interest in the armored suckermouth catfish of the Family Loricariidae. Although four genera, *Chaetostoma, Hypostomus, Rhineloricaria,* and *Sturisoma* have been recorded from Central America, the real center of the family's distribution is South America, home to 70 genera and over 500 species. The family comprises a number of species popularly regarded as "algae eaters" or, as they are better known in the trade, "glass cleaners." Aquarists sometimes make the disagreeable discovery that the "glass cleaner" has not only failed to perform its assigned task, but has treated its tank's ornamental planting as a salad bar, devouring it completely in a single night's grazing. Thus, it is important to carefully research a given loricariid species before bringing it home. Loricariid catfish differ markedly in temperament and, given how many different species are offered for sale under the labels "pleco" or *Ancistrus,* the risk that a newcomer will be confused with a better-known and behaviorally very different species is quite real.

The body shape of loricariids betrays their preference for rapidly flowing waters. The flattened body offers little resistance to the current, while the large, ventrally situated mouth acts like a giant suction cup, permitting them to cling securely to the bottom. The powerful tail provides propulsive force, while the dorsal fin acts as a keel to maintain the fish's equilibrium.

Loricariids are usually offered for sale at a size somewhere between 1 and 3 in (4 to 8 cm) long. At this size, some of these catfish are fully grown, such as the various species of the genus *Otocinclus,* which never grow larger than 2 in (5 cm) long. Others are mere babies, no more than a few weeks old. In two years' time, some of these catfish may well measure up to 1 ft (30 cm) long. Indeed, given a large enough tank and the right sort of food, some can grow to 2 ft (60 cm) long.

▲ *The royal whiptail (Sturisoma aureum) is the most elegant loricariid catfish.*

▲ *The gold nugget pleco, a Baryancistrus often sold under the code name L-18.*

▶ *Otocinclus affinis lives in small groups and requires fresh vegetable matter. If its aquarium lacks sufficient algal growth, it must be offered lettuce leaves and peas.*

◄ *Male* Ancistrus, *commonly known as bushy-nosed plecos (shown here is* Ancistrus temminckii) *can be recognized by the thick, fleshy barbels around their mouths and snouts.*

▶ *A native of Brazil, the gypsy king or tiger pleco (*Peckoltia sp.*) grows no more than 6 in (15 cm) long. As yet unidentified, this catfish bears the code name L-66, which allows scientists and aquarists to keep track of unidentified representatives of the family Loricariidae. New species are discovered almost daily.*

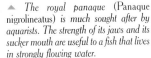

▲ *The royal panaque (*Panaque nigrolineatus*) is much sought after by aquarists. The strength of its jaws and its sucker mouth are useful to a fish that lives in strongly flowing water.*

▲ *The name of* Parancistrus aurantiacus *is somewhat misleading. Its specific epithet,* aurantiagus, *means golden, yet the fish is gray! Specimens change from gold to gray after a few days in captivity.*

▲ *Dietary roughage in the form of waterlogged wood is essential to the well-being of many loricariids, such as these* Scobiancistrus aureatus.

▲ *This mango pleco (*Parancistrus sp.*) is one of the numerous loricariids discovered within the past few years in the Xingu River.*

▼ *Many* Sturisoma *species (shown here is* Sturisoma rostratum*) conceal themselves in the substratum, so their tanks must be furnished with a thin layer of fine sand.*

▲ *Bulldog plecos are rather delicate and do not live long under aquarium conditions, probably because of inadequate diet. These fish demand strong water movement in their tanks, which must be equipped with powerful filters.*

◄ *The origins of* Rineloricaria sp./red *are a mystery. Is the fish a naturally occurring mutant of* Rineloricaria lanceolata *or the product of genetic manipulation in the laboratory? It prospers in captivity only if its diet includes fresh vegetable matter.*

Ouch!

Some loricariids possess bony plaques known as scutes that are formidably armed with hooks or sharp spines. Such accessory spines are often found on the cheeks, the bony first ray of the pectoral fin, and on the flanks. These structures appear to serve as both an antipredator defense and a secondary sexual characteristic in such genera as *Pseudacanthicus*. These fish should not be moved using nets, as the spines invariably get tangled in the mesh.

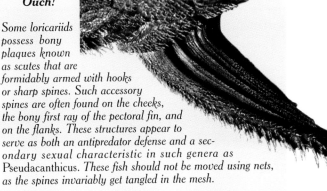

The Whisker Brigade

▲ *The striped Rafael catfish (Platydoras costatus), Family Doradidae.*

▶ *Catfish of the genus Synodontis (Family Mochokidae) are equipped with two pairs of extremely sensitive chin barbels that detect any movement in the substratum beneath them.*

▲ *The red-tailed catfish (Phractocephalus hemioliopterus) can grow to 5 ft (1.5 m) long. A giant predatory representative of the Family Pimelodidae, it needs its own aquarium.*

▼ *The naked catfish of the genus Pimelodus are encountered in schools of several thousand in the rivers of South America. Shown here is Pimelodus blochi.*

In addition to the representatives of the Callichthyidae and Loricariidae, a number of other catfish, scattered among several more or less familiar families, enjoy favor among tropical fish enthusiasts.

The waters of Africa and Asia shelter a number of species less readily available to hobbyists by virtue of their large size or lack of attractive coloration. Some of these catfish can survive in oxygen-deficient waters or even leave the water and move overland because of their highly branched superbranchial organs, accessory "lungs" analogous to the labyrinth organ of bettas and gouramis. Others can be dangerous to man. Only seven families out of the many known fish are capable of detecting and emitting electrical signals, notable among them mormyrids, rays, New World knifefish—and catfish.

While all of the latter have the necessary sense organs to detect electrical fields, their vestigial development makes it unlikely that most catfish can actually make use of this sensory modality. Among those fish that use electrical discharges to stun or kill their prey is one very dangerous catfish—the electric catfish (*Malapterurus electricus*) in Africa. This species can attain a length of 4 ft (1.2 m) and routinely emits electrical discharges of 100 to 300 volts, even up to 600 volts! Other catfish will attack any foot that inadvertently disturbs them, inflicting painful wounds with their sharp pectoral spines. Such behavior is well documented in the Asian mud catfish *Heteropneustes fossilis*.

Happily, the great majority of catfish, such as the African *Synodontis* species so familiar to aquarists, are perfectly harmless.

▲ *The Family Bagridae includes a number of large, highly predatory naked catfish, such as these representatives of an unidentified Auchenoglanis species.*

▶ *Aquarists appreciate the upside-down catfish (Synodontis nigriventris) for both its small adult size and its bizarre mode of swimming.*

▲ The Indian butterfly catfish (Hara hara) is a dwarf species of the Family Sisoridae, whose largest representatives can measure up to 6 ft (2 m) long.

▶ The Lake Tanganyika cuckoo catfish (Synodontis multipunctatus).

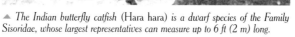

▲ Glass catfish (Kryptopterus bicirrhis) live in enormous schools. Despite their small size, these representatives of the Family Siluridae are caught and consumed as food in their native Southeast Asia.

▶ The large eyes of most Synodontis species betray their crepuscular activity. Shown here is Synodontis alberti.

▼ Albino specimens of the walking catfish (Clarias batrachus) are not that rare in nature. This representative of the Family Clariidae can live for a long time out of water and routinely moves overland between pools.

▲ Beware of the flattened snout and wide mouth (Sorubim lima). It is quite capable of engulfing sizeable prey. Smaller tankmates run the risk of being added to the menu as live food. This fish should be kept only by those hobbyists with very large tanks.

Cuckoo!

The reproductive pattern of Synodontis multipunctatus differs from that of other mochokid catfish. Consorting couples of S. multipunctatus interrupt consorting couples of mouthbrooding cichlids to concurrently deposit their eggs within the cichlids' spawning pit. The female cichlid takes them into her mouth along with her own eggs. The young catfish develop more rapidly than do their cichlid broodmates, hatching in three days. The young catfish then devour the developing cichlid embryos.

▼ Pangasius hypopthalmus is a midwater-swimming catfish with an extremely rapid growth rate.

▲ The most commonly available representative of the Family Aspredinidae, the banjo catfish (Dysichthys coracoideus) buries itself in the substratum up to its mouth. Prey that pass within striking distance are immediately snapped up.

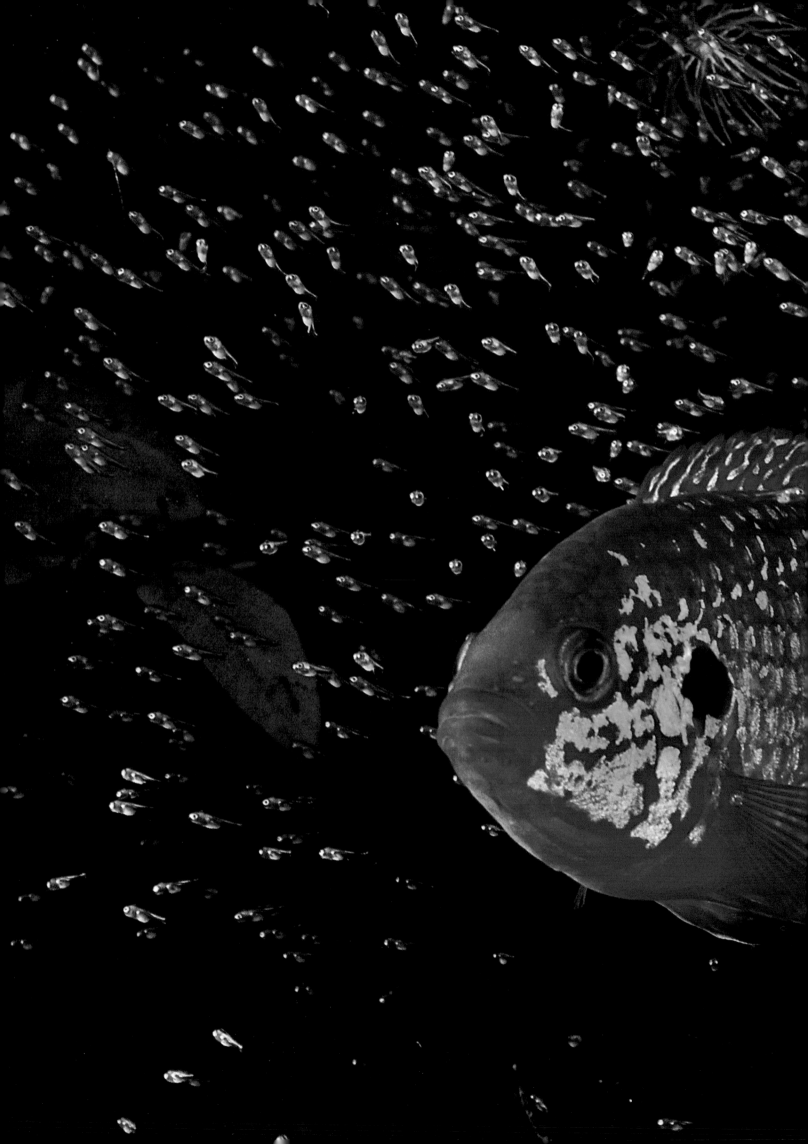

Attentive
Parents

Angelfish and Discus

▲ *This checkerboard discus is strangely colored.*

▶ *A wild-caught specimen of* Symphysodon aequifasciata.

▼ *This cross between a pigeon's blood and a turquoise discus is one of the Asian color varieties that have inspired aquarists' infatuation with these cichlids.*

The observation "Cichlids are killers" dates from the era of their first importation, when hobbyists added them at random to small community tanks containing peaceful, often shy, schooling fish. Today, such a course of action would be considered ludicrous, but it would be unfair for today's aquarium hobbyists to criticize too harshly the actions of their parents and grandparents. Fifty years ago, virtually nothing was known of the behavior and husbandry requirements of these very distinctive fish. It was largely thanks to the information garnered by the few scientific explorers of that era and the pioneering efforts of a handful of passionate enthusiasts that cichlids really won the approval of aquarists in the years between 1970 and 1980. The family's popularity is in large measure due to their complex reproductive behavior, which centers on highly evolved parental care of their young. Note: Cichlidomania is a highly contagious and quite incurable condition.

Angelfish and discus are certainly the most widely kept and eagerly sought-after cichlids. The first specimens of *Pterophyllum scalare* were imported from South America at the beginning of the twentieth century. This majestic fish possesses a remarkable amount of genetic variability, expressed in numerous color and finnage mutations. The price aquarists must pay for this diversity is a certain amount of irreversible genetic degeneration, manifested in reduced hardiness and the attenuation or complete loss of normal parental behavior in many aquarium strains of angelfish.

Discus were very much the province of an elite group of fish fanciers until large-scale commercial production in the 1990s of both wild form and selected color varieties of *Symphysodon aequifasciata* in Asia. The true or Heckel discus (*Symphysodon discus*) is restricted to the Rio Negro in Brazil. This species has evolved in water absolutely devoid of dissolved minerals whose pH oscillates between a dry season high of 5.0 and a rainy season low of 3.2. The difficulty of reproducing such conditions in the aquarium explains why the husbandry of the Heckel discus is best left to experienced breeders.

▶ *Young angelfish about five weeks old.*

▼ *A veiltail zebra angelfish.*

Discus "Milk"

Discus inhabit water so acidic that the microscopic animals that normally serve as food for the fry cannot survive in it. Discus have evolved a means of coping with this scarcity. Parental fish secrete a nutritious mucus that is an indispensable first food for their fry. This brown discus parades its month-old fry in a breeding tank.

▲ Discus can live quite satisfactorily in a community tank stocked with peaceful South American fishes.

▲ Young marble angelfish about three months old. This is the size at which angelfish are commonly offered for sale.

▼ Solid blue fish, such as these Rubin blue discus, are highly sought after by fish fanciers.

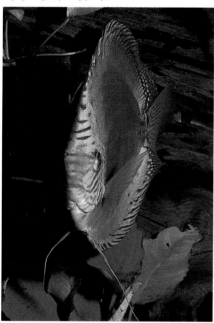

▲ A pair of the wild color form of Pterophyllum scalare guards their eggs on an Amazon swordplant.

▼ The red turquoise discus, with its wavy brick red stripes on a blue background.

▲ Unless their owner's objective is to breed them selectively, there is no reason why different color varieties of discus cannot be kept together.

▼ Ritualized combat between two male angelfish for the attentions of a female.

◀ The altum angel (Pterophyllum altum) is the king of all angelfish. Extremely difficult to breed in captivity, the rare specimens offered for sale are all wild caught.

▲ A half-black angelfish.

▲ The golden ram, a selectively bred color variety of Papiliochromis ramirezi, is susceptible to disease.

▲ Crenicichla compressiceps is a diminutive rheophile predator that barely exceeds 3 in (8 cm) in length.

▼ A well-planted aquarium is an absolute necessity for Crenicichla regani, a timid fish that likes shelter.

New World Dwarf Cichlids

The name dwarf cichlid is applied to any species whose adult size does not exceed 4 in (10 cm). The habitats of these fish are small West African and South American streams flowing under forest cover. Their unaggressive temperament makes them suitable candidates for a community tank. These fish live in the lower reaches of an aquarium, which should be heavily planted and well supplied with rockwork and waterlogged branches. Such hiding places are essential to their well-being and afford them spawning sites where they can keep their fry secure from the predatory attentions of their characin tankmates. The temperature of the tank's water, which should always be soft and acid, should fall somewhere between 74 and 86°F (27 to 30°C).

Sexual differences in finnage and coloration are usually well developed among dwarf cichlids. Males have longer fins and are more vividly colored than the females, which are rather drab except when tending eggs or fry. The closely related genus *Papiliochromis* comprises two species: *Papiliochromis ramirezi* requires very soft, acid water; *Papiliochromis altispinosa* prefers neutral to slightly alkaline conditions. *Laetacara* resemble diminutive *Aequidens*. Along with representatives of the related genera *Cleithracara* and *Nannacara*, they are frequently referred to as dwarf acaras. The larger congeners of the dwarf *Crenicichla* are formidable predators, many capable of growing over 12 in (40 cm) long.

Dwarf cichlids are either monogamous or harem polygynists, with many females sharing the territory of a single male. You must research the mating system of a given species carefully before purchasing it, or you may put the female's life in danger.

▲ Largely because it is so easily bred, the curviceps (Laetacara curviceps) is the dwarf acara best known to hobbyists. Here a female deposits her eggs on an Anubias leaf.

▲ Its distinctive color pattern has earned Cleithracara maronii the common name of keyhole cichlid.

▲ This young male golden-eyed dwarf cichlid (Nannacara anomala) is developing his iridescent golden green adult coloration.

◀ *The survival of the Bolivian ram* (Papiliochromis alti-spinosa) *is threatened by the grading of its habitat to facilitate cattle ranching.*

▼ *A pair of* Apistogramma viejita, *a dwarf cichlid native to Colombia, watches over its newly free-swimming fry.*

▼ *The acara bobo* (Laetacara dorsigera) *has wine-red coloration that darkens to black in sexually active individuals.*

▲ *The cockatoo dwarf cichlid* (Apistogramma caca-tuoides), *long confused with* Apistogramma borellii, *is one of the few species of the genus that lives and breeds in alkaline water.*

▼ *The distinctive coloration of male* Apistogramma nijsseni *made a star of this species in 1979.*

▲ *The sexual dimorphism in color pattern characteristic of the genus* Apistogramma *is exemplified by this parental female* A. nijsseni.

▲ *A spawning pair of rams* (Papiliochromis ramirezi). *Inducing this species to spawn is a simple matter, but rearing the resulting fry is not.*

▲ *An undescribed* Laetacara *species, related to L. curviceps.*

◀ *The coloration of male* Apistogramma agassizii *varies as a function of its locality of origin.*

▶ *Regardless of their origin, all female* Apistogramma agassizii *have essentially identical coloration.*

Large New World Cichlids

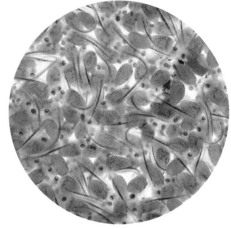

▲ *Most Central American cichlids can produce spawns well in excess of 1,000 eggs. The larvae depicted here are a week old.*

▼ *View of a spawning female* Theraps bifasciatus. *The ovipositer is wide and blunt to facilitate the passage of the eggs.*

▲ *A close-up of the genital papilla of a spawning male* Theraps bifasciatus *as he fertilizes the eggs.*

▶ *Many different populations of the firemouth cichlid (*Thorichthys meeki*) inhabit the waters of southeastern Mexico, eastern Guatemala, and Belize.*

▼ *A large aquarium is essential for* Amphilophus festae.

It is customary to group the large American cichlids according to their geographic origins, as this has a direct bearing upon their maintenance. One thus draws a distinction between the cichlids of Mexico and Central America, where hard and somewhat alkaline water is the norm, and those of South America, a region of soft, acid water.

Most of the fish until recently grouped in the genus *Cichlasoma* belong to the first group, mostly large fish in which both sexes are characterized by particularly vivid coloration. Many species can grow to 16 in (40 cm) in length; a few can exceed 31 in (80 cm). Noted for the intensity of their parental care, these fish are indefatigable gravel movers, their ability to dig directly proportional to their size. They usually select a spawning site in the open. It is not unusual for a female to lay as many as 3,000 eggs. After a few days, a swarm of fry swirls about the two parents that are ready to protect their progeny. A very large aquarium is necessary to properly care for these robust fish, which can weigh up to several pounds. A tank over 6 ft (1.8 m) long is barely large enough to allow four pairs of several different genera to coexist. Most of these fish are omnivores.

South America is home to many different cichlid lineages. In addition to dwarf cichlids, there are also many large species that can attain a length of 1 ft (30 cm) or more. *Aequidens* and *Geophagus* are two of the largest genera of South American cichlids. Most of these cichlids carry their developing embryos in their buccal cavities. In order to properly maintain these species in captivity, it is important to determine beforehand their preferred water chemistry. South America is a vast area and aquatic biotopes there vary markedly with respect to pH and hardness.

▶ *There are few reports of successful breeding of* Acarichthys heckelii *in captivity. In nature, a male maintains a harem of up to five females.*

▼ Paraneetroplus bulleri *is a rheophile cichlid native to northern Guatemala.*

▲ *The maintenance requirements of* Biotodoma wavrini, *a notably shy and delicate cichlid, are identical to those of the discus.*

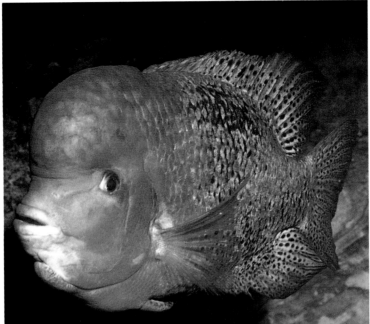

▲ The triangle cichlid (Uaru amphiacanthoides) resembles the discus in both the details of its behavior and its basic husbandry requirements.

▶ The quetzal cichlid (Theraps synspilus) is an outstanding Central American cichlid.

▼ Native to Guatemala, Herichthys bocourti is a species only a few of the world's cichlid enthusiasts can as yet hope to possess.

▲ With a large mouth and eyes placed high up on the head, Satanoperca leucostica can bury its snout deep in the sand when foraging for food.

▼ A large aquarium is absolutely essential for this female Amphilophus festae to avoid the unwanted attentions of her overly amorous consort.

◀ Juvenile oscars (Astro-notus ocellatus) easily win the hearts of inexperienced aquarists. Adults grow over 1 ft (30 cm) long.

▶ Different populations of green severum formerly classified as Heros severus are now known to be different and distinct species.

▼ The Midas cichlid (Amphilophus citrinellus) is best left to the cichlid specialist. This dominant male is capable of killing his mate in minutes.

▲ This female red-hump earth eater (Geophagus stein-dachneri) shelters her three-day-old fry in her buccal cavity. They seek their shelter at the slightest disturbance.

▲ A pair of a spectacular undescribed Crenicichla species native to the Xingu River. The female's red belly indicates that she is ready to spawn.

▲ *The king of Lake Tanganyika cichlids, the frontosa (Cyphotilapia frontosa) has converted many aquarists to cichlid keeping.*

Cichlids of Lake Tanganyika

▲ *The Tanganyikan cichlid Neolamprologus brichardi.*

▼ *The deep, laterally compressed body, large mouth, and highly protractile jaws of Altolamprologus compressiceps are all attributes of a formidable predator.*

H ome to nearly 200 species of cichlids found nowhere else in the world, Lake Tanganyika is an inexhaustible source of aquaristic novelties. The lake's cichlids continue to evolve. Separated by a physical feature such as a river mouth, a single ancestral population can give rise to two daughter populations that differ markedly in coloration. The outcome of this process can be seen in the many localized color varieties of *Tropheus moorii* and a number of *Neolamprologus* species.

Located near the midpoint of Africa's Great Rift, the lake measures nearly 400 mi (644 km) long but no more than 48 mi (77 km) wide. With a maximum depth of just over 4,800 ft (1,470 m), Lake Tanganyika is the world's second-deepest lake, but its cichlids live at depths of only 260 ft (79 m) or less. They can be found along rocky shorelines and over sand and mud bottoms along the lake's

1,200 mi (1,932 km) of shoreline.

Given tanks in the 50- to 60-gal (200 to 300 L) size range—or larger—the husbandry of Lake Tanganyika cichlids is relatively straightforward. Provided it is hard and alkaline, tapwater will satisfy the needs of these fish. A total hardness of 250 ppm closely approximates that of the lake's water. The pH should remain between 7.8 and 9.0, and the water temperature between 74 and 82°F (23 to 27°C). The tank bottom should be covered by a thin layer of fine sand and decorated with rockwork arranged in discrete formations. This decor can be softened with strategically placed stands of such tough-leafed aquatic plants as *Anubias* and *Vallisneria*.

A community tank of Tanganyikan cichlids is feasible, but to keep violence at a minimum, select only tankmates with different color patterns, lifestyles, and reproductive behavior.

▲ Julidochromis ornatus *is the best known and most widely available species of its genus.*

▲ *Male Lake Tanganyika featherfin cichlids such as this* Cyathopharynx furcifer *construct nest pits in the sand to entice ripe females for spawning.*

◀ *As its specific name* calvus *[= bald] suggests, the nape of* Altolamprologus calvus *is devoid of scales.*

▷ A pair of Neolamprologus gracilis defending mobile fry a few days old.

▽ A male Lamprologus ocellatus on guard at the mouth of his shell. Inside, his mate cares for a clutch of newly hatched fry.

▲ Gnathochromis perm-axillaris spends most of its time sifting mouthfuls of sand to extract the minute organism on which it feeds.

◀ Reciprocal threat behavior by both partners of a pair of Neolamprologus brichardi allows them to test each other's strength prior to spawning.

▽ Neolamprologus multi-fasciatus lives in extended family groups in empty snail shells.

▲ Neolamprologus cylindricus is small but quarrelsome. Success with this species requires only one pair per tank.

▷ Male Opthalmotilapia nasuta differ from females in their long ventral fins with their spatulate yellow-orange tips.

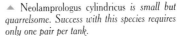

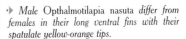

▲ Cichlids of the genus Petrochromis (shown here is a male of the Tofo population of Petrochromis polydon) have a wide mouth for rasping algae and their associated microorganisms from rocky surfaces.

▽ Callochromis macrops is a small, sand-dwelling cichlid.

▲ Tropheus duboisi usually lives in small groups over rocky bottoms. Success with this species entails replicating such social groups in very large tanks.

Juvenile Color Pattern

The color pattern of juvenile Troph-eus duboisi consists of iridescent blue-white spots on a velvety black back-ground. This coloration allows them to remain unmolested with a group's territory until they attain sexual maturity. Within a few weeks, the spots are replaced by an off-white vertical bar. Young males are then expelled from the group, which typically consists of a male and several females.

Cichlids of Lake Malawi

▲ A male red-shouldered peacock (Aulonacara hansbaenschi).

▶ Sunset on Lake Malawi.

▼ Although males grow to an impressive 7 in (18 cm), the sunshine peacock (Aulonacara baenschi) is relatively peaceful.

▲ A female Tyranochromis continues to watch over her 1-in-long (3 cm) young.

▲ A female Aulonacara jacobfreibergi, usually sold under the name Trematocranus jacobfreibergi, watchfully parades her fry.

▲ Aulonacara maylandi earns its common name of sulfur-head peacock.

Lake Malawi offers much of interest to aquarists and is home to endemic cichlids of astonishing coloration and exciting behavior. They are notable for their exemplary parental behavior. Their practice of maternal mouthbrooding places these cichlids securely in the ranks of the most highly evolved animals.

These cichlids can be divided into two groups, the haplochromines and the tilapiines, known locally as *chambo*. Best known of the haplochromines are the *mbuna*, or rockfish, active, vividly hued cichlids (blue and orange are the most commonly seen colors) that feed on the algal mat on the lake's rocky shoreline. The remaining members of the group have more or less tapered bodies, characterized by extreme sexual color dimorphism: males are luminous, females drab. Both haplochromines and Lake Malawi's endemic tilapiines are maternal mouthbrooders. The female carries her fertilized eggs in her mouth until they complete their development, a period of two to three weeks after spawning. Once they are fully developed, the female releases her brood in a spot that has appropriate food.

These cichlids are easily maintained, needing only a lot of swimming space. Some species grow over 1 ft (30 cm) long. Their water should be moderately hard, with a pH somewhere between 7.2 and 8.5. The tank must be well filtered. A temperature 75 to 78°F (about 25°C) suffices for day-to-day maintenance. An abundance of shelter, best provided by piles of large rocks, is greatly appreciated. Several stands of hardy, tough-leafed aquatic plants complete the tank's decor. The mbuna are predominantly herbivorous, but will take pelletized and most frozen foods. In captivity, even haplochromine species that feed primarily on insect larvae and other aquatic organisms benefit from the inclusion of vegetable foods. Feeding these cichlids a diet based upon meat and *Tubifex* worms can have lethal consequences.

▲ The yellow labido (Labidochromis cf. caeruleus) is among the most peaceful of the mbuna.

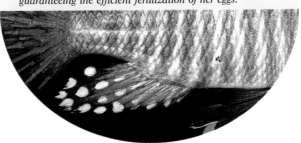

Egg Dummies

The males of many mouthbrooding cichlids possess one or more spots on the anal fin, usually about the same size and color as the eggs of the species. As the female bites at these egg dummies, she gets a mouthful of the male's sperm, guaranteeing the efficient fertilization of her eggs.

▲ The electric blue cichlid (Sciaenochromis fryeri), *highly prized for its coloration. Some specimens seem to be quite delicate; others have lived for ten years in captivity.*

▲ *This female Malawi blue dolphin cichlid (Cyrtocara moorii) is calling her fry back to the shelter of her buccal cavity.*

▲ *Despite its reputation as an eyeball eater, Dimidiochromis compressiceps can behave peacefully—barring the introduction of smaller companions.*

▲ *Its large, sensitive lips help* Placidochromis milomo *to detect its insect prey.*

▲ Melanochromis auratus *was one of the first mbuna species exported to Europe and North America in the mid-1960s.*

▲ *A hardy cichlid, the red empress (Protomelas cf. taeniolatus) is a good choice for the novice cichlid fancier.*

▲ *A female* Fossorochromis rostratus *shares a nursery tank with her two-day-old fry.*

◀ *A male* Nimbochromis venustus *requires a large tank to prosper.*

▲ *The rocky shore of Lake Malawi is home to many different geographic races of both* Labeotropheus trewavasae *and* L. fuelleborni. *Shown here is a male of the Thumbi Island population of* L. trewavasae.

▲ Pseudotropheus zebra *is best maintained on a harem basis, with one male per tank—unless one has access to a heated swimming pool.*

◀ *A female of the piebald or OB color morph of* Pseudotropheus zebra.

▶ A female giant krib (Pelvicachromis sacrimontis).

▼ A male Haplochromis sp. "flameback," which has contributed significantly to the current interest in Lake Victoria cichlids.

▲ Undescribed Lake Victoria cichlid widely sold under the erroneous name Haplochromis obliquidens or CH44.

▲ A female blue jewel fish. This artificially selected color form of Hemichrimis guttatus does not exist in nature.

▲ Hemichromis sp. "orange," a newly discovered undescribed species from Guinea.

▲ Native to the rapids of the lower Congo River, Steatocranus tinanti requires well-oxygenated water.

▲ Astatotilapia latifasciata, a recently imported haplochromine species native to Lake Kioga. The clear sexual dimorphism of this species is immediately evident.

The Cichlids of Africa's Rivers, Lake Victoria, and Madagascar

Lake Victoria, situated to the north of the two great Rift Valley lakes, is home to a diverse assemblage of cichlids, 95 percent found only there. Identifying Lake Victoria cichlids at the species level is complicated by complexes of morphologically very similar animals with relatively restricted ranges, so knowing where a given fish was collected is often the first step toward determining its identity. Lake Victoria haplochromines are just beginning to make their commercial debut. They are hardy, easily bred maternal mouthbrooders. The chief problem facing a prospective breeder is being certain of having both sexes of the same species.

The streams draining the rain forests of West Africa and the tributaries of the Congo River are home to a very different assemblage of cichlids. These streams contain many colorful species of modest size. The cichlids of the genera Hemichromis, Pelvicachromis, and Nanochromis frequent the leaf litter along the banks of these streams.

These waters are relatively soft and their temperature in full sun ranges from 77 to 83°F (25 to 28°C).

Aquatic vegetation is often abundant, offering these fish numerous hiding places.

The main channel of the Congo River and its major tributaries present a radically different biotope. Rapids and eddies follow one another in rapid succession. This is the preferred habitat of Steatocranus and Teleogramma cichlids. Well adapted to life in fast-moving water, these fish are characterized by elongate bodies and more-or-less atrophied swim bladders, making it easier for these fish to remain in contact with the bottom and avoid being swept away by the current. They live in the shelter of large boulders and in the cracks and crannies of the rocky debris along these river bottoms where they deposit their adhesive eggs.

It is widely accepted that the cichlids of Madagascar are living representatives of the family's most primitive known lineages. Regrettably, most of the island's cichlids, among them several recently discovered species, are at risk of extinction due to the effects of large-scale deforestation.

▲ *A male of an undescribed species of the* Pelvicachromis humilis.

▼ *The massive nuchal hump of the buffalohead cichlid (*Steatocranus casuarius*) is a distinctive attribute of sexually active males.*

▲ *The Mozambique mouthbrooder (*Oreochromis mossambicus*) finds virtually all water conditions to its liking. The more saline the water, the more intense the male's courting dress.*

▲ *A female common krib (*Pelvicachromis pulcher*) with her brood of fry. Colorful and easily bred, this species has introduced many aquarists to the wonderful world of cichlids.*

▲ *The marakely (*Paratilapia polleni*) is the best known of Madagascar's native cichlids. Other species, some only recently discovered, are on the verge of extinction.*

▲ *A male of the red color form of* Pelvicachromis taeniatus. *It is essential to avoid housing females of the different color forms together, as they are impossible to tell apart.*

A Biological Pollutant?

Aquarists began to take a serious interest in Lake Victoria toward the end of the 1980s. During the 1950s both the Nile perch (Lates niloticus) and the Nile tilapia (Oreochromis niloticus) were introduced to the lake in the hope of reestablishing viable commercial fishing. Ironically, the Nile perch has not found favor with lake dwellers, as it cannot be preserved using the methods available to them. The dramatic disappearance of native cichlids has been blamed on the Nile perch rather than on increased trawl fishing or the pollution of local waters by urban sprawl.

There seems little doubt of the impact of Nile perch predation on those cichlid species that lived in the pelagic zone or over open bottoms, but it seems unlikely that this explanation applies to the increasing rarity of small, formerly abundant rock-dwelling cichlids.

▲ *Male Sahel jewel fish (*Hemichromis letourneauxi*). Breeding males turn cherry red.*

▶ *Her throat distended with four-day-old embryos, this female* Haplochromis sp. *"flameback" "chews" them to assure them a steady supply of well-oxygenated water.*

Cold-water Fish

Koi

▲ *Although purists prefer to display koi in unplanted ponds, there is no reason why their quarters cannot be decorated with water plants as long as their roots are protected from disturbance by large slabs of rock.*

▼ *A koi pond at feeding time.*

The carp is the trademark fish of European fresh waters. Originally from central Asia, carp were introduced to Europe, where they now inhabit slowly moving and even quite stagnant bodies of water. This fish is appreciated by sport fishermen as it is important in aquaculture. Spawning takes place in May and June, when the springtime sun has raised water temperatures to around 65°F (18°C). Depending upon her size and weight, a female can spawn from 50, 000 to 1.5 million eggs. Under natural conditions, carp can grow to over 3 ft (1 m) long and exceed 70 lbs (30 kg).

Easily cultured and bred, carp were originally reared by Asian peasants as a source of high-protein food. Fish farmers soon began to notice unusually marked and colored individuals among their pond-bred fry. Over 1,000 years ago, breeders first began rearing carp as strictly ornamental subjects.

Known in English as fancy or colored carp, these fish are known to the Japanese as *nishiki-goi, higoi,* or *koi* (which means "love"). This last name is singularly appropriate, as in Japanese culture, the carp is a symbol of fertility. With their elegant form and vivid colors, koi are the unquestioned monarchs of any garden pond. Exceptionally fine specimens have sold for prices as high as $250,000.

There are over 100 name varieties of koi, differing in color pattern, the presence or absence of scales, their size and position, and the presence or absence of metallic iridescence in their base coloration. These qualities are always judged by observing the fish from above. The most highly esteemed variety is the *tancho,* whose color pattern duplicates that of the Japanese flag. The ideal tancho is a brilliant white fish marked with a perfect red circle on the forehead whose borders do not tough the eyes. The odds of obtaining such a specimen even in a brood produced by the most carefully selected parents explains the astronomical prices paid for perfect tancho.

Indeed, the odds are against obtaining quality specimens of any koi variety. Only 200 out of any 1,000 fry produced are even worth the effort of marketing. Of these, only 10 to 20 really deserve being called koi. It is not unusual to encounter 60-year-old carp; the oldest known documented koi is 256 years old, an age confirmed by the analysis of its scale rings. The nutritional needs of koi, as well as their oxygen requirements, dictate that they be housed in spacious ponds.

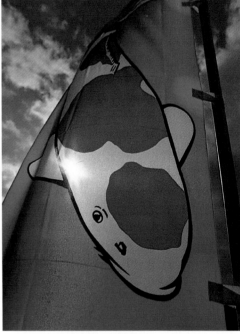

▲ *In much of Asia, and especially in Japan, the koi is highly venerated as a bearer of good fortune.*

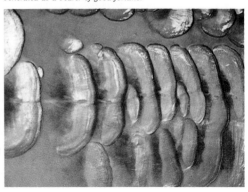

▲ *The flanks of the mirror carp are adorned with several rows of large, highly reflective scales.*

▲ *The wild color form of the carp (Cyprinus carpio).*

▶ *A leather carp, a scaleless variety with soft, velvety skin.*

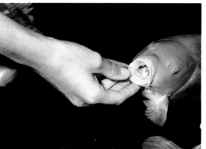

▼ A koi quickly learns to recognize the person who feeds it.

Tactile Barbels

The position of a fish's mouth reveals its feeding habits. That of the carp points downward, clear indication of a bottom feeder. The oral barbels allow the fish to detect buried food; the protractile mouth sucks in mud and invertebrates alike. The pharyngeal teeth macerate both impartially; the gill rakers separate food from inedible residue, ejected via the gill slits.

▲ When breeding carp, it is customary to offer them nylon mops as spawning sites. Infertile eggs can easily be recognized by their whitish color.

◄ Red and white fish comprise the majority of fish offered for sale in the Hong Kong koi market. These fish are customer favorites.

▶ Koi viewed from the side. Their distinctive color patterns are not shown to best advantage here.

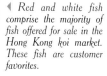

▲ A tancho gin matsuba.

▲ Left: a platinum doitsu; right: a platinum ginrin.

▲ A matsuba harewake.

▲ A kin matsuba.

▲ A kuchibeni kohaku.

▲ A shusui.

▲ A taisho sanke.

▲ *A black moor, common telescope-eyed goldfish.*

▶ *One cannot emphasize too strongly that fish should not be housed in goldfish bowls.*

▲ *The wild form of the goldfish,* Carassius auratus. *Neither body shape nor finnage are modified in any way.*

Goldfish

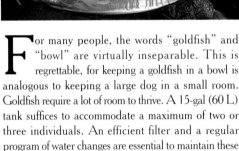

▲ *Size comparison of a two-week-old goldfish fry and a red ramshorn snail.*

▼ *Young specimens of the red cap oranda.*

For many people, the words "goldfish" and "bowl" are virtually inseparable. This is regrettable, for keeping a goldfish in a bowl is analogous to keeping a large dog in a small room. Goldfish require a lot of room to thrive. A 15-gal (60 L) tank suffices to accommodate a maximum of two or three individuals. An efficient filter and a regular program of water changes are essential to maintain these fish in good health.

The goldfish sold today bear little resemblance to their wild ancestors. The wild color form of the goldfish *(Carassius auratus)*, often confused with the crucian carp *(Carassius carassius)*, is a slender, silvery olive fish. In nature, it is not unusual to encounter in both lakes and rivers the occasional gold or red-orange individual. However, domesticated goldfish varieties differ from their wild progenitors in body shape and fin development as well as in coloration. As is the case with koi, fancy goldfish all have varietal names, such as oranda and shubunkin. Through selective breeding, a number of these fish

have gradually lost their dorsal fins, while the fins of other varieties are produced to form veritable veils. In other varieties, the body has become foreshortened and egg-shaped, or the eyes bulge from their sockets. While the results of such selective breeding are, as geneticists define the term, monstrous, the lively behavior of these fish remains undiminished, although the more highly modified fancy goldfish varieties do experience a certain amount of difficulty in swimming. Goldfish are long-lived; there are records of individuals living 20 to 40 years in Asia.

The first goldfish made their appearance in China during the twelfth century A.D. These fish rapidly assumed the status of domesticated animals and it was considered the height of fashion to display such fish in ceramic bowls, distant cousins of our aquaria. The first specimens to reach Europe arrived in England around 1600. The goldfish has continued to rise in the world and is now the most widely sold of all ornamental fish.

▲ *The comet, seen here, is a goldfish with a normal body but elongated fins.*

◄ *A well-formed telescope veiltail. Sometimes only one eye becomes enlarged.*

▼ *A telescope veiltail showing the shubunkin color pattern, with its mix of orange, white, blue, and black.*

▲ *The bubble-eye, with its characteristic fluid-filled subocular bladders, lacks a dorsal fin. The fish's swimming ability is seriously compromised by these bulging appendages.*

◄ *Tank specifically set up for fancy goldfish, planted with Anacharis, an aquatic plant that does well in cool water. Efficient filtration is essential for a tank housing these very messy fish.*

▲ *A black oranda, also known as a black tiger head goldfish in Japan. Its fleshy "cap" is the result of the tumor-like proliferation of skin cells.*

◄ *This superb and very high-priced show-quality oranda is the result of a cross between a lionhead and a veiltail. Its back is a uniform red color.*

▲ *The true lion head is completely bereft of a dorsal fin. This goldfish variety is very popular in Britain and Japan.*

◄ *A pearlscale goldfish, a variety defined by its mutated scale shape.*

▶ *The shubunkin is an attractive goldfish variety readily accessible to nonspecialists.*

◄ *The stand of a traveling koi and goldfish seller in Hong Kong.*

Other Cold-water Fish

▲ *A Japanese bitterling (Acanthorhodeus sp.).*

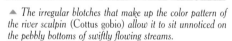

▲ *The irregular blotches that make up the color pattern of the river sculpin (Cottus gobio) allow it to sit unnoticed on the pebbly bottoms of swiftly flowing streams.*

▼ *The pumpkinseed (Lepomis gibbosus), a North American native, was introduced to Europe in the nineteenth century.*

Relatively few hobbyists show much interest in fish native to either cold or seasonally warm waters. Tropical fish offer a palette of color patterns that would justify their choice. Also, the large adult size of many native species makes it very difficult for amateur aquarists to house them properly. It is here that public aquaria again play an important educational role. Where else would one see superbly colored sunfish, yellow perch, or bitterlings if these institutions did not display them? To be sure, one can see trout, eels, and pike for sale at the fish market, but one must see these fish in life to appreciate their predatory behavior as well as the superb camouflage that insures the survival of the species.

One should set up an aquarium for cold-water fish as one would a tank for tropical species, paying particular attention to plants. Not all native species can tolerate either the constant 65 to 68°F (18 to 20°C). of the average home or nibbling of some native fish. Consult an appropriate reference work in order to best select appropriate plants, such as hornwort *(Ceratophyllum demersum)*, elodea *(Egeria densa)*, arrowhead *(Sagittaria subulata)*, water milfoil *(Myriophyllum* spp.), and eelgrass *(Vallisneria* spp.). In addition to the European species mentioned, some small fish native to Asia and North America are also appropriate candidates for such an aquarium. Many of these species, sold as tropical fish, have far shorter lives at temperatures between 77 and 82°F (25 to 28°C), and even display their most brilliant coloration at 68°F (20°C).

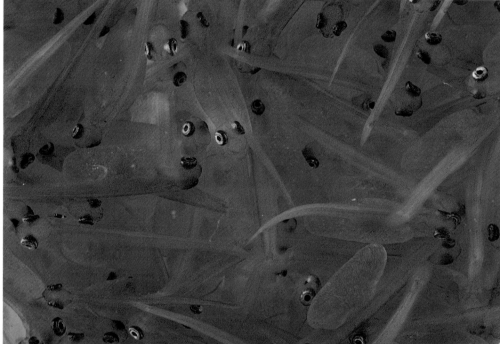

▲ *These salmonid larvae, only a few days old, have not yet fully absorbed their yolk sacs.*

◀ *Eels (Anguilla anguilla) spend their adult lives in fresh water, returning to the sea to breed.*

▼ *Growing no more than 3 in (10 cm) long, the black banded sunfish (Enneacanthus chaetodon) is both smaller and less aggressive than the pumpkinseed.*

Vampire!

These barbarous-looking instruments are nothing more than the teeth of the sea lamprey (Petromyzon marinus). Thus armed, it is child's play for this predator to attach itself to the flanks of its victim and either tear away its flesh or suck its blood. In either case, the victimized fish rarely survives its wounds. Public aquaria exhibit these predators by themselves in refrigerated display tanks.

▶ *The pike (Esox lucius) is an ambush rather than a pursuit predator. Its voracity has been greatly exaggerated. Pike usually make do with one meal a week.*

▶ *The eggs of the European perch (Perca fluviatilis), frequently observed in aquaria, are deposited in gelatinous ribbons.*

◀ *The coloration of the tench (Tinca tinca) varies according to the fish's surroundings.*

▲ *Armed with extremely sharp dorsal spines, the three-spined stickleback (Gasterosteus aculeatus) is often rejected as unpalatable by its predators.*

▼ *The brown trout (Salmo trutta fario) needs a large, well-oxygenated tank. Insufficient concentrations of dissolved oxygen can "drown" them.*

▲ *The rudd (Scardinus erythropthalmus) is markedly herbivorous. Unplanted quarters are strongly advised.*

▲ *Brook char (Salvelinus fontinalis) succumbs to asphyxiation at temperatures higher than 60°F (15°C).*

▶ *The bullhead (Ictalurus melas), a North American exotic, unlike the European eels (Silurus glanis), has four not six pairs of oral barbels.*

▲ *Native to the mountains of southern China, the white cloud (Tanichthys albonubes) can withstand winter temperatures as low as 40°F (5°C).*

Brackish
Water
Fish

▲ The four-eyed fish (Anableps anableps) likes to float just beneath the surface of a well-planted aquarium.

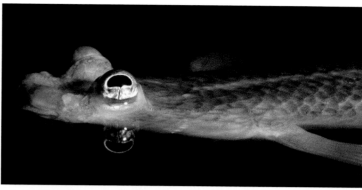

▲ In Anableps, each eye is divided into two discrete zones, allowing its possessor to see clearly both above and below the water.

▲ Sexually active adult male West African sleepers (Batanga lebretonis) can be recognized by their well-developed nuchal humps.

▶ The purple gudgeon (Mogurnda mogurnda) adapts equally well to fresh and brackish water.

▼ Beware of housing the spotted sleeper (Dormitator maculatus) in a planted tank; it will devour even their roots.

▲ The knight goby (Stigmatogobius sadanundio) must be kept in brackish water. It quickly develops skin ulcers when housed in fresh water.

Gobies, Puffers, and Similar Fish

The aquarium hobby is usually thought of as comprising the husbandry of either freshwater or marine fish. Relatively few of its devotees have any interest in brackish water—or to give them their proper name, euryhaline—fish. Contrary to popular belief, the term "brackish" does not refer to dirty, silt-laden water. Brackish waters are a mixture of fresh and seawater whose salinity in nature ranges from 1 to 25‰. The usually accepted range under aquarium conditions is from 5 to 20‰. This zone represents a transition between two radically different environments, a frontier that certain species of fish cross with impunity.

As a river approaches the sea, plant diversity decreases with progressively increasing salinity. There are a few plants that can tolerate low salinities. This affords an opportunity to vary the decor of a brackish water aquarium, which of necessity would otherwise be dominated by rockwork and waterlogged wood. Salt-tolerant species of genera Anubias, Bolbitis, Ceratophyllum, Ceratopteris, Cryptocoryne, Potamageton, and Vallisneria have been reported. These plants have been added to a brackish water tank after some hands-on tests of their resistance to saline conditions.

Gobiods are on the whole small fish and represent a good choice for the novice brackish water enthusiast, comprising over 2,000 species grouped into five families, of which the true gobies (Family Gobiidae) are the most important. True gobies, unlike the sleeper gobies (Family Eleotridae), have a vestigial swim bladder and hop rather than swim in the conventional sense. The teeth of all puffers are fused together to form a bony beak, a formidable weapon often employed with catastrophic consequences in an aquarium.

◀ Since the dusky sleeper (Eleotris fusca) is usually in fresh water in nature, it should be kept in such conditions in captivity.

Primitive?

Mudskippers are the only fish that routinely feed out of water. Insects, worms, even small crabs taken after molting their armor are their preferred foods. They carry a reservoir of water in their gill chambers and are able to modify their physiological state in order to reduce their body's need for oxygen. For such primitive animals, they are amazingly well adapted to their environment. Mudskippers' lifestyle demands that they be housed in a paludarium rather than a conventional aquarium, as they need a place where they can climb out of the water to rest and dig their burrows.

▲ The butterfly goby (Redigobius balteatus) moves upstream from estuaries in order to spawn in fresh water.

▲ The male bumblebee goby (Brachygobius xanthozona) cares for the eggs, usually deposited inside an empty snail shell.

▲ An Australian native, the desert goby (Chlamydogobius eremius) can withstand shifts in both water temperature and salinity.

▲ This male Amazon goby (Awaous flavus) spreads his colorful dorsal fin to attract a female.

▶ This 1/3-in-long (2 cm) dwarf puffer (Tetraodon sp.) is perfectly peaceful. It does not even nip its tankmates' fins.

▲ Despite its harmless appearance, the green puffer (Tetraodon fluviatilis) does not tolerate the presence of tankmates.

▲ The toadfish (Batrachus grunniens) growls when handled.

▶ The fins of the slender mudskipper (Boleopthalmus sp.) seem to have been painted by an artist. Seldom imported, this species is virtually unknown to aquarists.

▲ *The archer fish (Toxotes chatareus).*

▶ *A female of the golden variety of the orange chromide (Etroplus maculatus) with her two-day-old fry.*

From Pipefish to Moonies

▲ *Usually the size of a quarter when offered for sale, the silver moonie (Monodactylus argenteus) can grow to 10 in (25 cm).*

▼ *Adult Sebae moonies (Monodactylus sebae) are marine fish that breed in seawater, whose young mature in brackish water.*

▲ *Brackish or seawater suits the green chromide (Etroplus suratensis) equally well, but it does not prosper in fresh water.*

▼ *Listless and subject to numerous diseases when kept in fresh water, the spotted scat (Scatophagus argus) needs salt added to its tank.*

Just as a marine aquarist would never think of using table salt to replicate seawater, brackish water enthusiasts should always use one of the commercially available synthetic marine salt mixes when setting up their tank. These mixes contain the 50-odd trace elements the future inhabitants require to prosper. Hobbyists fortunate enough to live along the seacoast obviously have the option of collecting natural seawater from unpolluted areas.

Estuaries, salt marshes, and mangroves shelter fish whose adaptations to changing salinities are truly astonishing. Many of these fish must cope with tidal effects and must deal twice daily with the major osmotic stresses that follow in their wake. Other species move between environments at different stages of their life cycle. Notable among these are the amazing torrent gobies, which as adults live and spawn in the upper reaches of mountain streams, but whose larvae are carried by the current to the sea.

Many marine fish spawn in mangrove swamps, taking advantage of the shelter the roots of mangrove trees (*Rhizophora* and *Avicennia* spp.) offer their fry from predators. The sediments held in suspension by the currents that flow between them offer larval fish a far greater abundance and diversity of food than they would encounter in the ocean. It is depressing to see how estuaries have been treated as nothing more than receptacles for human trash, much of it industrial waste dumped into the water further upstream. In tropical countries, this fate has also befallen mangroves.

Archer fish should be housed in an aqua-terrarium that affords them sufficient headroom to practice their preferred pastime—hunting. These insect eaters capture their prey by "spitting" drops of water at insects that shelter in overhanging vegetation with sufficient force to knock them into the water.

The best-known Asian cichlids are representatives of the genus *Etroplus*, which are usually found in brackish water. The small orange chromide will live and breed in fresh water, but fry survivorship is greater when pairs spawn in brackish water.

The Siamese tiger perch (Datnioides microlepis) lives in the coastal waters of Southeast Asia. A large, fast-growing predator, it is best suited to the large tanks of a public aquarium.

The well-known mosquitofish (Gambusia affinis) controls mosquito populations in tropical areas by devouring their larvae.

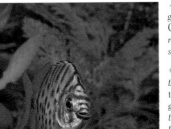

Many unidentified glassfish, such as this Chanda species, are routinely offered for sale.

The color pattern of the silver scat (Solenotoca multifasciata), elegant representative of the Scatophagidae, features spots and stripes.

The long filaments that adorn their dorsal and anal fins identify male Celebes rainbowfish (Telmatherina ladigesi).

The black-chinned tilapia (Sarotherodon melanotheron) is a mouthbrooding West African cichlid.

The mouth of the halfbeak (Dermogenys pusillus) is adapted to take prey from the water's surface.

The arching, stiltlike roots of the red mangrove tree (Rhizopora mangle), a defining feature of a mangrove swamp.

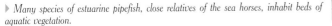

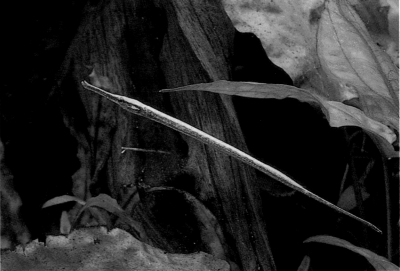

Mollies, whether black or sailfin, like the male Poecilia latipinna shown here, are more resistant to disease when a bit of salt is added to their water.

Many species of estuarine pipefish, close relatives of the sea horses, inhabit beds of aquatic vegetation.

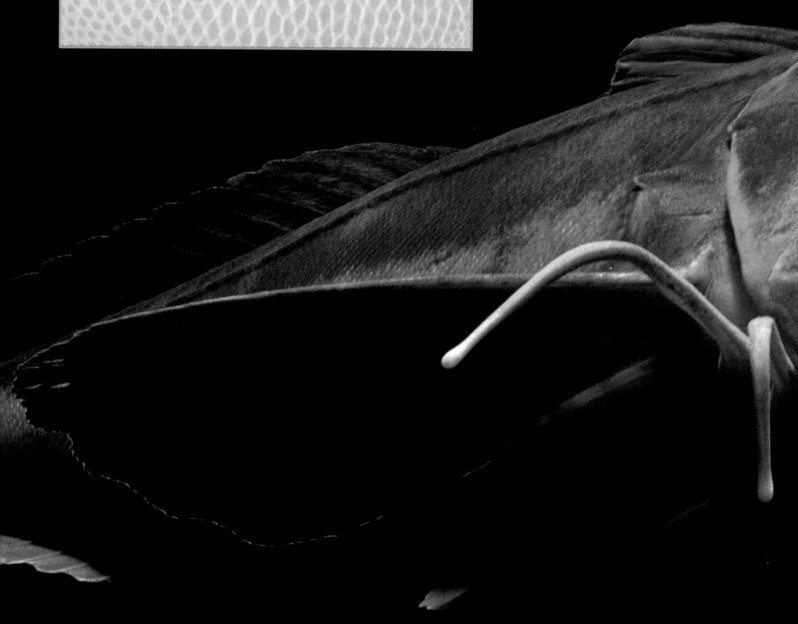

▲ *The color pattern of the female black-faced blenny (Tripterygion delaisi) is undistinguished, but males are colored an intense yellow.*

Blennies, Gobies, and Other Rock Dwellers

Maintaining an aquarium devoted to Europe's native marine fishes is not an easy task. Only species found in the intertidal zone or, in the case of Mediterranean species, that live close to shore and that can tolerate water temperatures that may sometimes rise above 77°F (25°C) are suitable candidates for hobbyists' tanks, unless they are willing to invest in a chiller system. Given their more elaborate life support systems, public aquaria are best suited to display native marine fish.

Tide pools support a highly distinctive community of organisms. Numerous species of algae have colonized these basins and many different animals either allow themselves to be trapped there or else enter them willingly. These include fry in search of food, the strayed young of pelagic species, and most notably blennies and gobies, permanent residents characterized by rudimentary swim bladders. Their buoyancy thus reduced, they can more effectively resist the action of breaking waves. Indeed, the fins in some families have the form of sucking disks, enabling the fish to cling to the rocks. Gobies and blennies that abandon their tide pools are restricted to rocky bottoms and are never found below a depth of 30 ft (9 m). At this depth, sufficient light penetrates to support the macroalgae whose associated community of epiphytic organisms provides these fish with their main source of food.

◀ *The cirrhi above the eyes of this tompot blenny (Parablennius gattorugine) are the mark of a sexually active male.*

▼ *The head of this breeding male red-faced blenny (Tripterygion tripteronotus) turns deep black.*

◀ *The tompot blenny is particularly partial to shore pools, where food is to be found in abundance.*

▼ *The coloration of the shanny (Lipophrys pholis) varies according to the bottom upon which it rests. Its thick lips are typical of this species.*

▲ *A color pattern consisting of a black stripe on a pale beige background hardly serves to camouflage this Roux's blenny (Parablennius rouxi).*

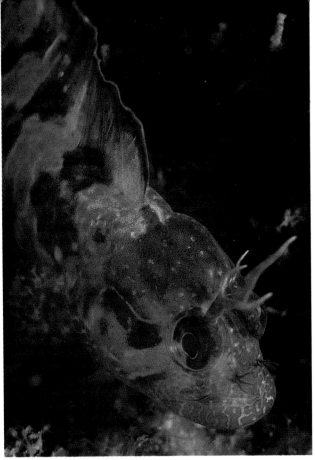

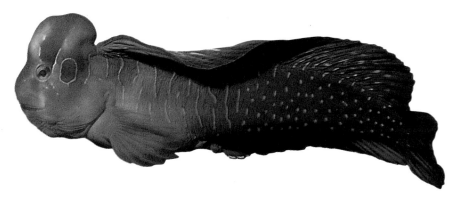

▲ *The peacock blenny (Salaria pavo).*

◀ *The male Pontic blenny (Parablennius incognitus) defends his nest, where females have deposited their eggs.*

▼ *A close-up portrait of a male peacock blenny, clearly showing his spectacular frontal crest.*

▲ *Ordinarily colored a nondescript beige, this male black goby (Gobius niger) shows off his velvety black breeding dress.*

▼ *The small-headed clingfish (Apletodon dentatus) grows no more than 2 in (5 cm) long.*

▲ *A distinctive characteristic of natural history of the two-spotted goby (Gobiusculus flavescens) is its predilection for leaving the shelter of the rocks to swim near macroalgae.*

◀ *Gobius cruentatus has earned its common name of bleeding or red-mouthed goby.*

▼ *The three-bearded rockling (Gaidropsarus vulgaris) forages at night and hides in cracks in the rocks during the day.*

▲ *The long-spined bullhead (Enophrys bubalis) resembles a diminutive scorpionfish.*

A Topsy-turvy World

Clingfish can attach themselves firmly to a rocky substratum with their highly modified paired fins, which function like suction cups. Individuals, such as this shore clingfish (Lepadogaster lepadogaster), often adhere to the underside of a rock. Males have puffy cheeks, an amusing secondary sexual characteristic.

73

In the Sand

▲ *Both the striped red goatfish* (Mullus surmuletus), *here photographed in the Mediterranean, and the red goatfish* (Mullus barbatus) *are highly esteemed food fish.*

▶ *At rest on a sandy bottom, the turbot* (Psetta maxima) *is virtually undetectable.*

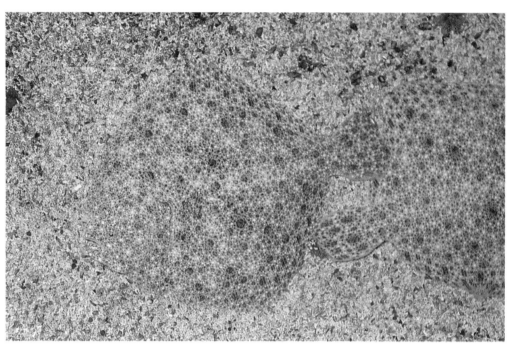

▲ *Goatfish possess a pair of long barbels on their chins with which they dislodge the small organisms they feed on from the sand.*

▲ *The red gurnard* (Chelidontichthys cuculus) *feeds on small fish and crustaceans it snaps up while skimming over the bottom.*

▲ *The gray gurnard* (Eutrigla gurnardus) *is the most attractive representative of the Family Triglidae.*

▶ *The brill* (Scolopthalmus rhombus) *is more oval than the turbot. This species can grow to 30 in (80 cm).*

Sandy or muddy bottoms harbor many small animals: worms, crustaceans, mollusks, and other potential prey. These vast submarine expanses are continually scoured by flatfish and other species capable of unearthing buried prey, such as the gurnard, which possesses specialized food-detecting organs. In effect, the tips of the unattached first three rays of the pectoral fins are supplied with specialized chemosensory organs. The motion of these rays conveys the impression that the gurnard is walking as it grubs in the sand. Gurnards also produce audible sounds from the swim bladder, which acts as a resonating chamber.

Flatfish are not usually displayed in aquaria, although most hobbyists are quite familiar with such species as the sole, dab, and turbot. Most flatfish have similar lifestyles, feeding primarily on small crustaceans, worms, and bivalves. A notable exception is the halibut, a predator that can grow to nearly 10 ft (3 m) long and actively pursues all kinds of fish at depths of up to 3,000 ft (1,000 m).

In flatfish, both eyes are on the same side of the head. During their larval stage, these fish swim in an upright position and have one eye on each side. Eventually, the fish begins to swim on its side. The eyes then migrate so that both end up on the same side. In the case of the turbot and the brill, both eyes are on the left side of the head; in the plaice and the sole, they are on the right.

Flatfish are habitually found in water up to several hundred feet deep. Like other deep-water residents, they can be properly displayed only in the large, refrigerated display tanks of public aquariums.

▶ *The pattern of blue pigment on the pectoral fins of the tub gurnard (Chelidontichthys lucerna) sets it clearly apart from the red gurnard.*

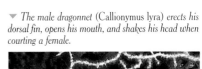

▼ *The male dragonnet (Callionymus lyra) erects his dorsal fin, opens his mouth, and shakes his head when courting a female.*

▲ *Gurnards—shown here is the streaked gurnard (Trigloporus lastoviza)—have the first three rays of the pectoral fin modified to form fingerlike structures that allow them to detect hidden prey as they "walk" over the bottom.*

▼ *With the help of its supple fins, the topknot (Zeugopterus punctatus) can adhere equally well to the top or underside of any solid object.*

▲ *The ventral surface of a common sole (Solea solea) lacks both pigment and its eye.*

▶ *The distorted face—typical of flatfish—of a fluke (Platichthys flesus).*

▲ *The ability of this Callionymus sp. to match its background is so perfectly developed that the fish is very hard to spot.*

Camouflage Dress

Round orange spots allow us to distinguish between a plaice and a dab (Limanda limanda). The spots of the latter are both less conspicuous and less regularly arrayed on the flanks.

▲ *The first spines of the dorsal fin of the weaver (Trachinus draco), which is furnished with poison glands, can inflict painful wounds.*

▼ *The plaice (Pleuronectes platessa) can also be found in the brackish waters of estuaries.*

Secondary Males

Fish characterized by extreme sexual dichromatism formerly posed a real puzzle to fishermen and ichthyologists. On the basis of their initial and terminal color patterns, individuals of the same species were often thought to represent different species, even without taking transitional color phases into account. Patient observation has solved many of the mysteries surrounding the sex lives of the most common of these fish. Shown here is a terminal phase male, formerly known as a regal rainbow wrasse.

▲ *The brown initial color phase of the Mediterranean rainbow wrasse (Coris julis) indicates either a female or an untransformed male.*

▲ *Because of its lack of aggressiveness, the rock wrasse (Ctenolabrus rupestris) is one of the easiest wrasse species to keep in an aquarium.*

▶ *This male Symphodus ocellatus is keeping exemplary watch over his nest of algal filaments.*

▼ *A painted comber (Serranus scriba).*

▲ *The ornate wrasse (Thalassoma pavo) is fond of warmth and does well in a tropical community tank.*

Wrasses and Serranids

▲ *The pearly razorfish (Xyrichthys novacula), named for its razor-thin body, is rarely encountered in nature.*

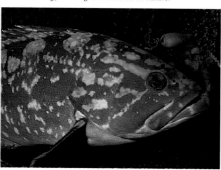

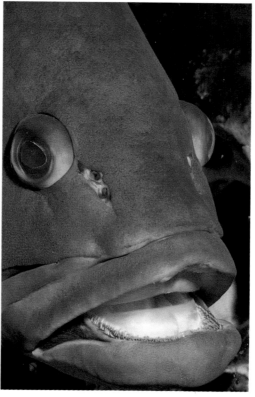

▲ *The speckled coloration of the female phase of the dusky grouper (Epinephelus marginatus).*

▶ *This dusky grouper now sports the uniformly dark coloration of a male.*

Wrasses and serranids are definitely the most beautiful European marine fish.

The reproductive biology of these fishes is extremely interesting. The scribbled sea bass, for instance, is a synchronous hermaphrodite. An individual possesses functional male and female sex organs and is theoretically capable of fertilizing its own eggs. However, the usual pattern observed in nature is for an individual to select a spawning partner and alternate between the male and female roles. Groupers, on the other hand, are sequential hermaphrodites, starting life as females and changing into males when they are several years old. Groups of these fish congregate in the neighborhood of underwater grottos. The black grouper is now strictly protected from human exploitation. The groups of young fish reported by sport divers in the Mediterranean are the fruits of this effective policy of protection.

Labrids such as the cuckoo wrasse and the Mediterranean rainbow wrasse change from female to male at four to five years of age. These fish frequent rocky shores, where they live in association with algal mats of beds of *Posidonia*. They are nowhere abundant.

▲ *This female cuckoo wrasse (Labrus bimaculatus) exemplifies the extreme differences between male and female coloration in this species.*

◀ *The extreme variability (green, yellow, or red) of the color patterns of individual Ballan wrasse (Labrus bergylta) is unrelated to their sex.*

▼ *The male cuckoo wrasse is more vividly colored than many coral reef fishes.*

▲ *Fishermen are well acquainted with the European sea bass (Dicentrarchus labrax), which can be caught in brackish waters as well as in the ocean.*

◀ *The similarity between the swallow-tail sea perch (Anthias anthias) and its tropical cousin the sea goldfish (Pseudanthias squamipinnis) is striking.*

▼ *Its uniformly spotted coloration distinguishes the mottled grouper (Mycteroperca rubra) from the female phase of the dusky grouper.*

▲ *The wide terminal mouth of the painted comber (Serranus scriba) betrays its predatory instincts. Its tankmates must therefore be selected very carefully.*

◀ *The range of the comber (Serranus cabrilla) extends to the coasts of the English Channel.*

Sea Breams and Scorpionfish

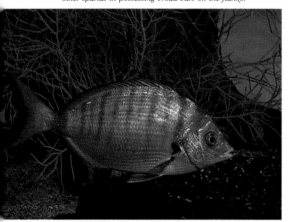

▲ *The zebra sea bream* (Diplodus cervinus) *differs from other sparids in possessing broad bars on the flanks.*

▲ *The narrow vertical bars of this young sharp-snout sea bream* (Diplodus puntazzo) *will disappear as it grows older.*

▼ *The white sea bream* (Diplodus sargus) *is very fond of sea urchins, which it cracks open with its powerful molars.*

Unscrupulous fish venders lump many silvery gray species under the heading of sea bream, so white sea bream are offered for sale at almost the same price as gilt-head sea bream. Members of the Family Sparidae, the common sea bream, the gilt-head bream, the black sea bream, the striped sea bream, the saddled sea bream, the pandora, and the salema inhabit the southern coasts of Europe, moving between the brackish waters of estuaries and the open sea. They live in highly structured schools and feed on smaller fish, mollusks, crustaceans, and occasionally, algae. Their pharyngeal jaws have massive molars with which they easily crush the shells of their prey.

Solitary and sedentary, scorpionfish are poor swimmers. This explains their highly cryptic color patterns, which are so often fatally deceptive to smaller fish. Scorpionfish are usually encountered at depths of 60 ft (20 m) or more, often perched on a rock, waiting to suck their prey into their mouths. At these depths, the red and yellow wavelengths have entirely disappeared, so the illumination is a soft blue. The red and brown coloration of most scorpionfish thus appears as shades of dark gray, which camouflages them very well. In addition to closely matching its background, the red scorpionfish has spines on its dorsal fin equipped with venom glands.

▲ *A common two-banded sea bream* (Diplodus vulgaris) *cruises over a carpet of* Posidonia *along the coast of Corsica.*

▶ *A close-up view of the impressive mouth of the red scorpionfish* (Scorpaena scrofa).

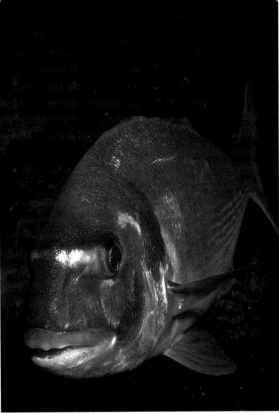

◀ *Shellfish and crustaceans—with that diet, it is hardly surprising that the flesh of the gilt-head bream (Sparus auratus) is highly regarded by seafood lovers.*

▶ *The red-banded sea bream (Pagrus auriga).*

▼ *The rosy coloration of the common pandora (Pagellus erythrinus) is more evident in a seafood store than in the living fish.*

▲ *Salema (Salpa salpa) begin life as males, then become females. They are common inhabitants of Posidonia beds.*

◀ *The common dentex (Dentex dentex) can grow up to 4 ft (1.2 m) long, the largest of the sparids.*

▼ *The small red scorpionfish (Scorpaena notata) grows to only 8 in (20 cm).*

▲ *The common sea bream (Sparus pagrus) is frequently marketed under the name of gilt-head. If sold as fillets, the buyer will probably be taken in by this deception.*

▶ *The black scorpionfish (Scorpaena porcus), an essential ingredient of bouillabaise, is less intensely colored than the red scorpionfish, but it is possible to confuse the two species.*

▼ *The scorpionfish shown here appears to be a member of the Scorpaenopsis gibbosa species complex.*

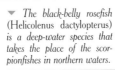

▼ *The black-belly rosefish (Helicolenus dactylopterus) is a deep-water species that takes the place of the scorpionfishes in northern waters.*

From Conger Eels to Torpedos

The wolf fish (Anarhichas lupus), *a fish of cold, deep waters, cracks open sea urchins with its powerful teeth.*

The boarfish (Capros aper) gulps down its prey with the aid of its amazingly protrusible jaws.

The snipefish (Macrorhamphosus scolopax) uses its long snout to grub through muddy bottoms. This fish makes a shrill noise when removed from the water.

With their bright blue coloration, juvenile Mediterranean chromis (Chromis chromis) are every bit as attractive as any tropical damselfish.

The yawn of this John Dory (Zeus faber) reveals the intricate mechanism of its highly protractile jaws.

A relative of the common cardinal fish (Apogon imberbis), the twinspot cardinal fish has two dark bars on the posterior half of its body.

The gray triggerfish (Balistes carolinensis) is the only representative of its family found along European shores.

A large assortment of species live along the coasts of Europe or in adjacent seas. The diversity of littoral biotopes is thus matched by that of the superbly adapted fish that inhabit them.

Algal mats and beds of sea grass growing in water less than 3 ft (91 cm) deep are the domain of the Family Syngnathidae, whose best-known representatives are the sea horses. Their ability to camouflage themselves is truly marvelous. As one descends further, eel-like fishes begin to appear in rocky crevices. Conger and moray eels show only their heads but are ready to launch themselves, jaws agape, at passing prey. Eels forage mainly at night, when they emerge from their shelters and hunt in the open. Rays and dogfish wander over sandy bottoms. Like sharks, these fish lack a bony skeleton. They are thus placed not in the Class Osteichthys (bony fish) but rather in a class of their own, Chondrichthys (cartilaginous

fish). In these fish, the bony elements of the skeleton are replaced by a framework of cartilage, which increases their buoyancy by reducing their weight. Some sharks swim constantly, for they must continually force a stream of well-oxygenated water over their gills. Unlike bony fish, many sharks do not have mobile gills.

The sharks that prowl along the coasts of Europe are for the most part small fish, although a few predatory species can grow up to 18 ft (6 m) long. A few very large species, such as the basking shark (Cetohinus maximus) are regular visitors to European waters. It is also worth noting that the great white shark (Carcharodon carcharias) has previously been reported from the Mediterranean Sea, which it enters through the Straits of Gibraltar. These fish are hardly appropriate aquarium subjects, although efforts to display them are presently underway in Japan.

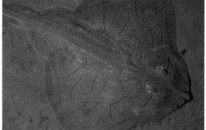

It is difficult to spot a painted ray (Raja undulata) resting on the bottom. Its intricate color pattern is only evident when it is illuminated by a photoflash.

◀ *A view of the underside of a thornback ray (Raja clavata) reveals its paired nostrils (not its eyes!), its mouth, and its gill slits.*

This common stingray (Dasyatis pastinaca) swims with nearly the elegance of a manta (Manta birostris).

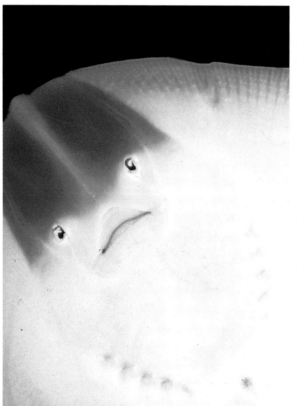

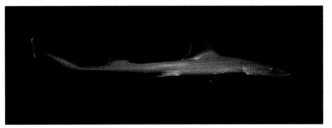

▲ As is the case with sea horses, it is the male snake pipefish (Entelurus aequoreus) that incubates in a ventral pouch the eggs deposited by the female.

▲ The starry smouthhound (Mustelus asterias) prefers to forage over muddy bottoms. Females give birth to live young.

◀ Thanks to its prehensile tail, this short-snouted sea horse (Hippocampus hippocampus) can keep a grip on this gorgonian.

▶ The common sea horse (Hippocampus ramulosus) can be recognized by the dermal filaments along its dorsal surface.

◀ The conger eel (Conger conger) can reach a length of 7 ft (2 m). It shares rocky crevices with the moray eel.

The Fair Helen

Alas, the Roman practice of feeding slaves or inept servants to the morays is not just a legend. The banquets of the powerful of that era were all the more appreciated if they included a dish of morays fed on human flesh. This close-up of the head of a common moray (Muraena helena) clearly shows its formidable teeth. The wounds they inflict are not only painful but quickly become infected.

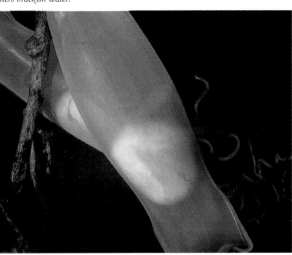

▲ Like many of its tropical cousins, the greater pipefish (Syngnathus acus) regularly enters brackish water.

▶ With its pattern of circular, white-edged blue spots regularly disposed along its disk-shaped body, doesn't this greater torpedo ray bear some resemblance to a UFO?

▲ The lesser spotted dogfish (Scyliorhinus canicula) lays eggs. The rosy developing embryo can be seen attached to its enormous whitish yolk sac.

▶ In addition to its greater adult size—5 ft (1.5 m) versus 30 in (80 cm)—the nursehound can be recognized by the spots that dominate its color pattern.

The Colors
of the Reef

Blennies, Gobies, and Dottybacks

Coral reefs support by far the most species of any aquatic biotope, either fish or invertebrates, which number in the thousands. These reefs are nearly 50 million years old. The great majority of the fish inhabiting coral reefs are members of the Order Perciformes. Among other features, these fish are all characterized by protractile jaws and well-developed pelvic fins. Their daily preoccupation is the search for food, either by preying upon smaller fish or by searching out small organisms concealed among the corals. Most of these fish are regularly marketed as aquarium residents. Establishing a mini-reef aquarium is the essential first step toward the successful husbandry of the smaller species. Its water should be of excellent quality, and the tank should be equipped with both a protein skimmer and a surge generator in order to better duplicate the essential features of the reef environment.

Coral reef blennies either have very small scales or else lack them entirely. The skin of these scaleless species is covered by a thick layer of protective mucus, hence their common appellation of "slimy" or "drooling" blennies. Like blennies, gobies are virtually incapable of swimming normally due to their poorly developed swim bladders. This adaptation to bottom dwelling has allowed a number of species to enter into a symbiotic relationship with blind burrowing shrimp. The goby mounts guard while the shrimp excavates their common burrow. In exchange for the shelter, the goby provides the shrimp with food.

The Microdesmidae, a family of fish closely related to the Gobiidae, differ from them in the extreme elongation of the rays of the first dorsal fin and in their more slender bodies. These fish can swim quite well and typically face into the prevailing currents, which carry the zooplankton upon which they feed.

The species available to aquarium hobbyists are all quite small, with maintenance requirements quite similar to those of previously cited families. Some pseudochromids are known to be mouthbrooders.

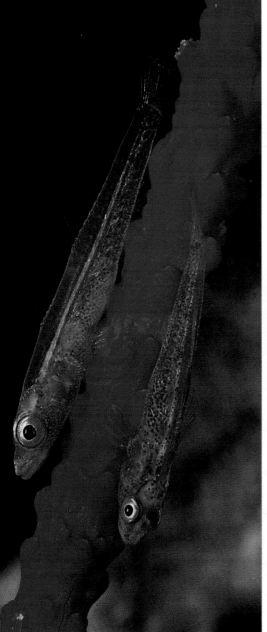

▲ Only an averted eye betrays the presence of this dwarf black coral goby (Bryaninops youngei), whose color pattern otherwise perfectly matches its invertebrate background.

▼ The branches of a gorgonian serve as a perch for these dwarf gobies (Bryaninops amplus).

▲ The striped blenny (Meiacanthus grammistes) leads a solitary life in the shallows of lagoons.

▼ One of the most attractive blennies in the aquarium trade, the Midas or golden blenny (Ecsenius midas).

▲ Despite its common name, the bicolor blenny (Ecsenius bicolor) is often uniformly maroon in color.

▼ The African blenny (Meiacanthus mossambicus) behaves aggressively toward congeners.

▼ The lemon goby (Gobiodon citrinus) rarely grows larger than 1 in (4 cm) long in captivity.

▼ Like all reef-dwelling gobies, the yellow coral goby (Gobiodon okinawae) requires the shelter of living invertebrates.

▲ The wide mouth and thick lips of the blue-striped goby (Valenciennea strigata) reveal it to be a sand sifter.

◀ Like many other gobies, the banded watchman goby (Ambyeleotris randalli) generally lives as pairs.

▶ This yellow watchman goby (Cryptocentrus cinctus) surveys its burrow, inhabited by a shrimp symbiote.

▲ The male firefish (Nemateleotris magnifica) erects his tall dorsal in order to intimidate rivals.

▲ Nemateleotris such as the purple firefish (Nemateleotris decora) use their dorsal fin to cram into rocky crevices.

▲ The lined dottyback (Labracinus lineatus) strongly resembles a small grouper. It reaches a length of 10 in (25 cm).

▲ Essentially solitary fish, pseudochromids such as this purple dottyback (Pseudochromis porphyreus) do not tolerate the presence of conspecifics.

▲ The zebra dart fish (Ptereleotris zebra) needs to live in a group in order to feel at ease.

Minute Missles

The morphology of dottybacks reveals an amazing ability to move at high speed. Quick starts to seize prey or attack a rival are part of the daily routine of these supposedly shy fish. As is the case with all of these fish, the fewer hiding places they are offered, the less frequently they will be seen. These fish are usually solitary, but at least one species, Springer's dottyback (Pseudochromis springeri) has been observed living as pairs, even outside of the breeding season.

▲ An easily maintained species, the false gramma (Pseudochromis paccagnellae) is sometimes referred to as the strawberry-vanilla dottyback.

▲ A chromis native of the Great Barrier Reef (Chromis nitida).

▶ Best-known representative of the genus, the common clownfish (Amphiprion ocellaris) will live in close association with an anemone if the latter is large enough to accommodate it. This species is often confused with Amphiprion percula.

▲ This chocolate clownfish (Amphiprion akyndinos) is inspecting his newly hatched fry.

▼ Its host anemone appears to have wrapped this skunk clown (Amphiprion akallopisos) in its gigantic tentacles.

▲ This pair of twin-banded clownfish (Amphiprion bicinctus) was photographed in its natural habitat in the Red Sea.

Clownfish and Damsels

Lolling about in the cozy bed afforded by its commensal anemone (a dozen species of the genera *Entacmaea*, *Heteractis*, and *Stoichactis* are especially favored), the clownfish leaves its shelter just long enough to snap up a hapless prey carried past by the current. One does not need an immense tank to properly house a pair of clownfish and their anemone.

Several of the 27 known species of clownfish will breed freely in captivity if they are well nourished and due attention is paid to water quality in their tank. The eggs are deposited in a rock or one of the sides of the aquarium, always near the pair's protective anemone. Both parents fan the clutch with the pectoral fins. The fry will take only the smallest of live foods. As *Artemia nauplii* are too large and indigestible to serve as a first food, cultures of microalgae and marine rotifers must be maintained to satisfy the appetite of the newly hatched larvae. The largest individual of a pair or group of clownfish is the female. Should she disappear, the dominant male will metamorphose into a female

and his place will be taken by the next largest individual in the group.

Damsels are the first fish divers see when they duck their heads beneath the surface of the tropical sea, for these are curious and often belligerent little fish. The Family Pomacentridae comprises many different genera, which can differ in body shape and color pattern. All damselfish deposit their eggs on a solid substratum, where they are tended by their parents until they hatch. In order for the species to survive, only two individuals out of all the eggs produced by a single pair need to survive to maturity.

▼ The tomato clownfish (Amphiprion frenatus) is one of the hardiest and most easily bred species of the genus.

◀ The base color of Clark's clownfish (Amphiprion clarkii) ranges from dusky orange to black, depending upon its point of origin.

▶ Nearly 6 in (14 cm) maximum, the saddle clownfish (Amphiprion ephippium) is one of the largest species of the genus. Juveniles resemble the common clownfish.

Clownfish hybridize freely in captivity. Shown here are the progeny of a cross between Amphiprion ephippium *and* A. frenatus, *nestled in the arms of a* Heteractis magnifica.

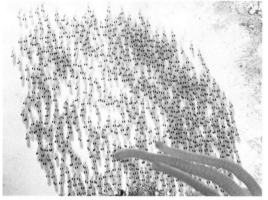

In an aquarium, the larvae have already developed an immunity to the stings of their parents' host anemone, which keeps them from being trapped by its tentacles when they hatch and rise into the plankton.

The three-spot damsel or domino (Dascyllus trimaculatus) *loses its white spots and becomes a solid reddish-brown fish when adult.*

Sergeant-majors are almost all marked with black vertical bars on a clear gray background. Here a group of convict damsels (Abudefduf vaigiensis) *hovers over a reef in the Red Sea.*

Its fluorescent blue coloration makes the Andaman Island neon damsel (Pomacentrus alleni) *a much sought-after but seldom available addition to a marine aquarium.*

Commensalism

The association of clownfish and anemone is usually refered to as symbiotic. This term signifies not only that each partner affords some benefit to the other, but that each is indispensable to the other's survival. As this is clearly not the case in the present instance, it is preferable to refer to this association as an instance of commensalism.

If one separates a clownfish from its host anemone for a few days, it will lose its immunity to attack and be treated like any other potential prey item by the anemone's stinging cells. As for the anemones, they are perfectly capable of capturing their own food. Nevertheless, they appreciate the presence of guests capable of defending them from the attacks of such coelenterate eaters as butterfly fish.

A Maldive clownfish (Amphiprion nigripes) *in its anemone* (Heteractis magnifica), *which has just closed around a prey item.*

There are many different color variants of the blue damsel (Crysiptera cyanea). *This yellow-throated male hails from Palau.*

The maroon clownfish (Premnas biaculeatus) *is the only species in its genus. It "inhabits" the anemone* Entacmaea quadricolor.

The green chromis (Chromis viridis) *is one of the most popular damselfish.*

This young Garibaldi (Hypsypops rubicunda) *superficially resembles a Chromis species, but will grow to over 24 in (35 cm) as an adult!*

Butterflyfish

▲ *The threadfin butterflyfish (Chaetodon auriga) exists in two color forms, one native to the Red Sea, the other widely distributed throughout the Indo-Pacific region.*

▶ *The raccoon butterflyfish (Chaetodon lunula).*

▲ *The Andaman Sea population of the common butterflyfish (Chaetodon plebius) lacks the species' trademark blue spot.*

As soon as divers enter the blue waters of a tropical lagoon, the first fish they notice are damsels, which seem to have colonized every available nubbin of coral. Their eyes are next drawn to the butterflyfish, omnipresent residents of coral reefs and the seas that bathe them. Swimming alone, in pairs, or in the case of some species, in schools, these brightly hued fishes are impossible to overlook as they move jerkily through the water. This unique and seemingly uncoordinated style of swimming has won these fish their vernacular designation of butterflyfish. The Family Chaetodontidae comprises about 115 species divided among a dozen genera. The family name is derived from the Greek *khaité* [= bristle] and *odon* [= tooth] and refers to their teeth, so fine that they can be compared to rigid hairs. Averaging between 5 and 6 in (12 to 15 cm) in length (the largest species rarely grow more than 8 in [20 cm] long), butterflyfish make ideal marine aquarium residents as long as their dietary requirements can be easily satisfied.

Nature has endowed butterfly fish with an extremely effective passive defense mechanism. The eye is a critically important sense organ for fish. Predators are well aware of this and often direct their attacks at their potential victim's head. Butterflyfish typically mask their eyes with a broad black stripe, and to further confound predators, many species have a large, round black spot, known as an ocellus, quite visible on the caudal peduncle or at the base of the soft dorsal fin. These fish have a false eye. A predator that strikes at this decoy not only does little damage to its intended victim, but is startled to see it shoot off at high speed—in reverse gear!

▲ *Juvenile specimens of the Chaetodon capistratus, four-eyed butterflyfish, have a second eyespot in the dorsal fin.*

▼ *The collared butterflyfish (Chaetodon collare) is found in abundance along the coast of Pakistan.*

▲ *The sickle band butterflyfish (Chaetodon falcula) is a resident of the Maldive Islands and is unquestionably one of the easiest butterflyfish to keep successfully in captivity.*

◀ *It is quite evident that the Ulithi Island butterflyfish (Chaetodon ulietensis) has many features in common with Chaetodon falcula. It differs from that species in the size and shape of its lateral bands and its shorter snout.*

▼ *The blue-striped butterflyfish (Chaetodon fremblii) is endemic to the Hawaiian Islands.*

▲ *A large species by family standards, the saddleback butterfly-fish (Chaetodon ephippium) can exceed 8 in (20 cm) in length.*

▶ *While it may live either as a solitary individual or in small groups, Klein's butterflyfish (Chaetodon kleini) is never found in large schools. It is a hardy aquarium resident.*

▼ *The lined butter-flyfish (Chaetodon lineolatus) is the largest species of the genus.*

▲ *The yellow-snouted butterflyfish (Chaetodon flavirostris) is notable for living in estuaries as well as on the reef.*

▼ *The checkered butterflyfish (Chaetodon rafflesi) sports a latticework color pattern.*

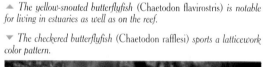

▼ *A common species in the Maldives, Meyer's butterflyfish (Chaetodon meyeri) boasts a highly distinctive color pattern that precludes confusing it with any other species.*

▲ *The black-back butterflyfish (Chaetodon melanotus) feeds primarily upon live coral polyps, and thus is not suited to life in captivity.*

▲ *A pair of dot and dash butterflyfish (Chaetodon pelewensis) wanders over a Polynesian reef.*

◀ *Growing to barely 4 in (10 cm) long, the spot and stripe butterflyfish (Chaetodon punctatofasciatus) is a rarely imported dwarf species.*

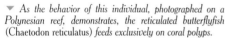

▲ Because it feeds on algae and small crustaceans, Rainford's butterflyfish (Chaetodon rainfordi) does well in captivity.

▼ As the behavior of this individual, photographed on a Polynesian reef, demonstrates, the reticulated butterflyfish (Chaetodon reticulatus) feeds exclusively on coral polyps.

▲ The relatively drab coloration of the banded butterflyfish (Chaetodon striatus) has few admirers among aquarists.

▼ The pastel butterflyfish (Mesochaetodon trifasciatus) has been moved to a new genus because its body is more ovoid in shape than that of other butterflyfish.

Butterflyfish (continued)

The long snouts of most butterflyfish leave few doubts as to their specialized manner of feeding. With mouths situated at the end of these "beaks," they poke around the branches of coral formations in search of small worms, crustaceans, and algae. This sort of dietary specialization does not make it easy to acclimate butterflyfish to captivity. This is particularly true of species with extremely specialized dietary requirements. Some of these feed only on sponges, others on live coral polyps. Needless to say, long-term maintenance of these species under aquarium conditions is virtually impossible. Unfortunately, these fish are still often offered for sale. Captured by fishermen who know nothing of their dietary requirements, and exported by individuals for whom a fish's well-being is the least of their concerns, these fish are condemned to certain death. Before purchasing any butterflyfish, it is absolutely imperative to fully research its dietary requirements. Among the hardiest butterflyfish are *Chaetodon kleini*, *Chaetodon lunula*, *Chaetodon collare*, *Chaetodon uletensis*, and a number of *Heniochus* species. *Chaetodon semilarvatus*, *Chaetodon falcula*, *Chaetodon auriga*, and *Chelmon rostratus* are best left to advanced hobbyists. *Chaetodon meyeri*, *Chaetodon ornatissimus*, and *Chaetodon xanthocephalus* are species to avoid at all costs.

◀ The progressive disappearance of the ocellus from the soft dorsal fin of this juvenile highfin butterflyfish (Coradion altivelis) sets it apart from Coradion chrysozonus and Coradion melanopus. The dorsal ocellus is a permanent feature of its congeners' color pattern.

▲ A common Red Sea species, the yellow butterflyfish (Chaetodon semilarvatus) is not easily acclimated to life in captivity.

▼ The pearlscale butterflyfish (Chaetodon xanthurus) is often confused with other members of its species complex, such as the orange butterflyfish (Chaetodon paucifasciatus).

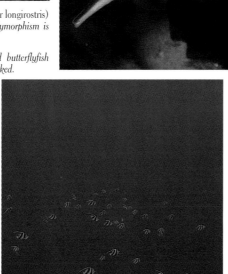

▲ Some individuals of the longnosed butterflyfish (Forcipiger longirostris) are chocolate brown in color. The reason for this color polymorphism is unknown.

▶ Close-up portrait of the head of the yellow longnosed butterflyfish (Forcipiger flavissimus). Note how the eye is completely masked.

▲ The pyramid butterflyfish (Hemitaurichthys polylepis) typically lives in schools of several hundred individuals.

Ex-Chaetodons

The species of the genus Chelmon were, with the longnosed butterflyfish (Forcipiger), formerly included in the genus Chaetodon. They were moved because of anatomical differences, notably the elongation of their snouts. This allows these fish, whose mouths are at the end of a tube created by the distortion of the jawbones, to forage within the branches of coral colonies for prey inaccessible to shorter-snouted butterflyfish. The copperband butterflyfish (Chelmon rostratus) conceal their true eye and draw attention to a clearly defined black ocellus in the soft dorsal fin.

▲ The wimplefish (Heniochus acuminatus) lives close to the reef, either by itself or in pairs.

▶ As this photo, taken at Ras Mohammed, clearly shows, Red Sea wimplefish always live as pairs. These two individuals are crossing the territory of several red argus groupers (Cephalopholis miniata).

▲ Sociable wimplefish (Heniochus diphreutes), like these specimens in the Maldives, live in large schools that are often encountered in midwater.

▼ The brown whimplefish (Heniochus monoceros) sports one protuberance in front of its eyes and another on its nape. This pair is in an aerated aquarium decorated with bright red synthetic coral.

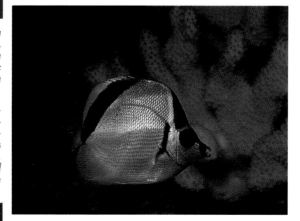

▲ Commonly known as the barber fish, Johnrandallia nigrirostris, like the cleaner wrasses, removes patches of dead skin and ectoparasites from other inhabitants of the reef.

▲ The genus Chelmonops (shown here is Chelmonops truncatus) bridges the gap between the genera Chaetodon and Chelmon.

Pygmy Angelfish

▲ *Lamarck's swallowtail angelfish (Genicantus lamarck) has four distinct color patterns, which differ in the number and width of its lateral stripes. Shown here is a male.*

▼ *Geniacanthus species (shown here, a female of Watanabe's swallowtail angelfish [Geniacanthus watanabei]) feel at ease in a well-decorated aquarium that offers them plenty of hiding places.*

Only a short time ago, angelfish and butterflyfish were considered to represent two subfamilies (Pomacanthinae and Chaetodontinae) of the single Family Chaetodontidae. While these two groups are closely related, angelfish are easily recognized by virtue of the large spine at the base of the gill cover. The Family Pomacanthidae comprises 75 species placed in nine different genera. Hybrids between a number of species have been documented. These fish are protogynous hermaphrodites: They all start life as females and eventually metamorphose into males, as do groupers. Under the heading of pygmy angelfish are species of the genera Centropyge and Geniacanthus. Centropyge species range from 2 to 5 in (5 to 12 cm) in length and feed primarily upon algae and small invertebrates. While clearly territorial, under natural conditions they live in groups. Unless you have access to a very large aquarium, you should house a single specimen of a given species per tank, although you can keep two specimens of different species together if their coloration differs markedly.

Growing somewhat larger than Centropyge, the elegant swallowtail angelfish of the genus Geniacanthus are notably more slender and possess a deeply emarginate caudal fin. The coloration of males and females differ so radically that for many years they were often described as distinct species. These fish feed primarily upon algae, zooplankton, and small invertebrates. Geniacanthus species are rarely imported.

▲ *Dramatic sexual dimorphism is seen in the genus Geniacanthus, as in this male Watanabe (Geniacanthus watanabei).*

▼ *Male zebra swallowtail angelfish (Geniacanthus melanospilus) possess narrow lateral bars lacking in females.*

▼ *The African pygmy angelfish (Centropyge acanthops) is abundant along the coasts of the Indian Ocean.*

▼ *Undemanding in its food preference, the cherubfish (Centropyge argi) adapts well to captivity.*

▼ *A bicolor pygmy angelfish (Centropyge bicolor) with its distinctive blue nuchal spot.*

▲ Eibl's pygmy angelfish (Centropyge eibli).

▲ The flame angelfish (Centropyge loriculus) does well in captivity but is fearful of more active tankmates.

▲ Difficult to acclimate, Potter's pygmy angelfish (Centropyge potteri) is best left to advanced hobbyists who can supply it with a wide selection of live foods.

▲ The Samoan race of Herald's pygmy angelfish (Centropyge heraldi) possess a black submarginal stripe in the soft dorsal fin lacking in other populations of this species.

▲ With its deep body and unusual profile, the banded pygmy angelfish (Centropyge multifasciatus) strongly resembles a Chaetodontoplus species.

▲ The rounded belly of this female resplendent pygmy angelfish (Centropyge resplendens) suggests she is about to spawn.

▲ Male rusty pygmy angelfish (Centropyge ferrugatus) can be recognized by the blue margins of their dorsal and anal fins.

▲ The yellow pygmy angelfish (Centropyge flavissimus) is extremely intolerant of the presence of other fish and will even pick fights with larger tankmates.

▶ Just over 2 in (6 cm), the Hawaiian pygmy angelfish (Centropyge fisheri) is the smallest species of the genus.

▲ The intensity of the blue coloration of the twinspine pygmy angelfish (Centropyge bispinosus) varies considerably from one individual to the next.

▲ *This threespot angelfish (Apolemichthys trima-culatus) is being groomed by a cleaner wrasse (Labroides dimidiatus).*

▶ *The regal angelfish (Pygoplites diacanthus) exists in two geographically distinct color forms. Apart from the presence of a large blue ocellus in the soft dorsal fin, juveniles look exactly like adults.*

▲ *Bright golden yellow with a large black ocellus on the flanks, a juvenile rock beauty (Holocanthus bicolor) resembles a Centropyge species.*

▼ *Like other representatives of the genus Chaetodontoplus, the vermiculated angelfish (Chaetodontoplus mesoleucus) is difficult to maintain under aquarium conditions.*

Large Angelfish

With their brilliant colors and imposing size—sometimes almost 2 ft (60 cm) long—angelfish are the royalty of the reef. These fish as a rule are either solitary or else live in pairs. Highly territorial, they do not tolerate the proximity of other species of the family.

A peculiarity of these fish is the astonishing difference between their juvenile and adult color patterns. The base color of juveniles is either black or dark blue, against which a pattern of straight, curved, or even circular lines is clearly visible. This coloration may perhaps serve to identify juvenile angelfish as potential cleaner fish. The young of many species have been observed in nature removing ectoparasites from other inhabitants of the reef, behavior that disappears concurrently with the juvenile coloration. This age-related difference in coloration also facilitates cohabitation of juveniles and adults.

In captivity, the rule is one angelfish per tank, which should have a volume of at least 125 gal (500 L). Angelfish are often very specialized feeders, eating primarily sponges, bryozoans, and algae. *Pomacanthus paru* is one of the easiest angelfish to acclimate to life in captivity; *Pygoplites diacanthus* is one of the most difficult. Juveniles of all species usually adapt better to captivity than adults, which often refuse to accept new foods.

▲ *Juveniles of the admiral angelfish (Euxiphipops navar-chus) adapt readily to life in captivity.*

▶ *The adult color pattern of the gold-spot angelfish (Apole-michthys xanthopunc-tatus) has made it highly sought after, though it is rarely imported.*

▲ *When diving in the Maldive Islands, it is not unusual to encounter a pair of yellow-naped angel-fish (Euxiphipops xantho-metopon).*

▶ *The strong opercular spine typical of the family is clearly visible in this monocled angelfish (Chae-todontoplus conspicillia-tus).*

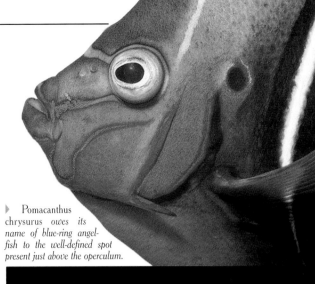

Natural Hybrids

There is a certain amount of confusion over the status of the queen angelfish (Holocanthus ciliaris) and the blue angelfish (Holocanthus bermudensis), shown in the adjacent photo. The juvenile coloration of the two species is virtually identical, which often results in young blue angelfish being sold as queen angelfish. Furthermore, over much of their broadly overlapping ranges, the two fish hybridize freely, giving rise to individuals of an intermediate color pattern, which are often marketed under the name Holocanthus ciliaris. To further confuse matters, the name Holocanthus isabelita, synonym of Holocanthus bermudensis, is often erroneously used in the aquarium literature instead of the valid name. Fortunately, this has little practical significance, as there is no risk of hybrids being propagated for the aquarium trade.

▷ Pomacanthus chrysurus owes its name of blue-ring angelfish to the well-defined spot present just above the operculum.

▲ Juvenile gray angelfish (Pomacanthus arcuatus) and French angelfish (Pomacanthus paru) are virtually indistinguishable. Adults of the former, shown in the photo above, are pale gray, while those of the latter are black with yellow-edged scales.

◁ French angelfish may reach a length of nearly 20 in (50 cm) in the wild.

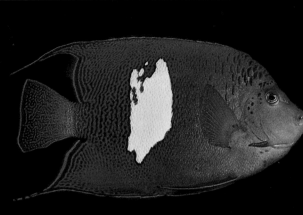

▷ This subadult passer angelfish (Holocanthus passer) will gradually lose the narrow blue lines on its flanks.

▲ The crescent angelfish (Pomacanthus maculosus), depicted above, is often confused with the asfur or halfmoon angelfish (Asuretta asfur). The shape of the yellow spot on the flanks is the best way to tell them apart.

▲ Juvenile emperor angelfish (Pomacanthus imperator) are marked with a series of concentric white, sky blue, and midnight blue circles that radiate outward from the caudal peduncle.

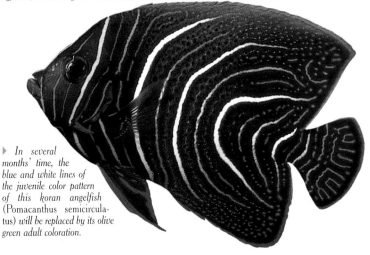

▲ This adult queen angelfish (Holocanthus ciliaris) shows a pattern that clearly differs from that of the juvenile fish (see photo at right).

▷ Juvenile queen angelfish readily accept the usual selection of foods offered to aquarium fish; adults will often starve rather than change their diets.

▷ In several months' time, the blue and white lines of the juvenile color pattern of this koran angelfish (Pomacanthus semicirculatus) will be replaced by its olive green adult coloration.

▲ *A Japanese white-cheeked surgeonfish (Acanthurus japonicus). This fish, whose color pattern resembles that of Acanthurus glaucopareius, lives in large schools.*

▶ *Once it has successfully completed the difficult process of adjusting to life in captivity, the powder blue tang (Acanthurus leucosternon) is a good choice for a solitary existence.*

Surgeonfish and Tangs

▲ *Provided it is offered a large tank, the lined tang (Acanthurus lineatus) is the perfect choice for the aquarist with no prior experience of surgeonfish.*

▼ *The Achilles tang (Acanthurus achilles) is not a good beginner's choice. The vivid orange area immediately surrounding its scalpel serves to deter potential enemies.*

▼ *The sohal tang (Acanthurus sohal) lives on shallow, often wave-battered reefs.*

Surgeonfish are a feature of all tropical seas. The Family Acanthuridae comprises approximately 70 species grouped into 6 genera. These fish range from 8 in (20 cm) to just over 3 ft (1 m) in length. Their name is from the scalpellike blades located at the base of the caudal fin, a formidable weapon. A blow of the tail suffices to slash the flank of a conspecific adversary or of an aggressor of another species. These blades are highly modified scales. In most surgeonfish, they are concealed within a slit and erected when danger threatens. The scalpel of the several *Naso* species is fixed in place and its blade directed anteriorly. As a rule, the area immediately around the blade is vividly colored, as if to dissuade potential adversaries. Imprudent sport divers have had the veins of their wrist slashed as a result of trying to insert it into a school of surgeonfish.

With the onset of breeding, these fish gather in large groups. Males and females cautiously leave the larger group and swim rapidly toward the surface. As they do so, the decrease in ambient pressure causes their swim bladders to expand. The pressure thus exerted on the gonads causes the male and female to simultaneously expel sperm and eggs into the water column. The floating eggs hatch approximately 24 hours later. The resulting young eventually develop into *Acronurus* larvae, characterized by long, venomous dorsal and anal fin spines.

Surgeonfish and tangs are easily maintained in captivity. Powerful swimmers, these fish require large tanks to prosper in captivity. Housing certain species together—*Acanthurus lineatus* and *Acanthurus sohal*, for example, is not advisable. These fish feed on algae, which they crop with their spatula-shaped teeth. Despite conventional wisdom, surgeonfish do not eat coral polyps. They play an important role in maintaining the health of a mini-reef tank by preventing the proliferation of noxious algae.

▲ *Juvenile orange-shouldered tangs (Acanthurus olivaceus) are colored bright yellow.*

◀ *Although easily maintained, the white-tailed surgeonfish (Acanthurus xanthopterus) is suited only for life in very large tanks, as it can grow over 20 in (50 cm) long.*

◀ Acanthurus glaucopareius and Ctenochaetus striatus grub among coral heads on this Polynesian reef in search of the algae and minute invertebrates that make up their diet.

▶ To encounter a zebra unicorn tang (Naso vlamingi) over 2 ft (70 cm) long while diving in Polynesia is an unforgettable experience.

▼ A problem encountered when unicorn tangs (Naso brevirostris) are kept in aquaria is a tendency for them to damage their "horn." This specimen has had its length reduced by half.

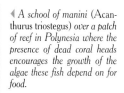

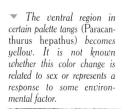

▲ The color pattern of the orange-spurred surgeonfish (Naso lituratus) varies from one locality to the next.

◀ It is essential to purchase only juvenile specimens of the yellow tang (Zebrasoma flavescens), for adults adapt poorly to life in captivity.

▼ Cleaner shrimp (Lysmata amboinensis) grooming a zebra sailfin tang (Zebrasoma veliferum) that has assumed a stereotypical posture.

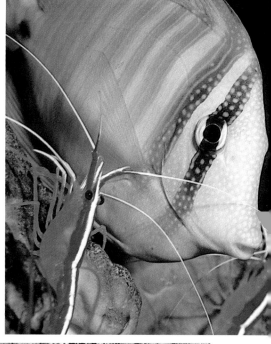

▲ The sailfin tang (Zebrasona desjardinii) is often confused with the closely related zebra sailfin tang (Zebrasona veliferum) despite the presence of specific characteristics that allow for the recognition of each.

◀ A school of manini (Acanthurus triostegus) over a patch of reef in Polynesia where the presence of dead coral heads encourages the growth of the algae these fish depend on for food.

▼ The ventral region in certain palette tangs (Paracanthurus hepathus) becomes yellow. It is not known whether this color change is related to sex or represents a response to some environmental factor.

◀ The rusty orange coloration of this Hawaiian tang (Ctenochaetus hawaiiensis) will gradually turn brown as it matures.

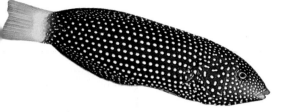

▲ *The female phase of the Guinea hen wrasse (Anampses meleagrides).*

▶ *Juvenile Cuban hogfish (Bodianus pulchellus), are, like many wrasses, facultative cleaner fishes.*

▲ *Like other wrasses, the Diana hogfish (Bodianus diana) requires many hiding places to feel at ease in captivity.*

▼ *The yellow juveniles of the black-banded hogfish (Bodianus bilunulatus) are marked with a dark lateral bar that extends from the dorsal to the anal fin.*

▼ *The Spanish hogfish (Bodianus rufus) can grow to 1 ft (30 cm) long in captivity but attains twice that length in nature.*

Wrasses

On all of the world's coral reefs, wrasses are among the most easily recognized of all fish thanks to their elongate, slender form. They are also among the best represented. Most adult wrasses live as solitary individuals, but do not hesitate to form small breeding groups as the occasion warrants. As is the case with those representatives of the family native to cold waters, adult females eventually change into males. Juveniles are typically colored very differently from such terminal males. These differences in color pattern are particularly striking within the genus *Coris*, which explains why for many years these different color phases were thought to be different species. These fish feed on small invertebrates, such as mollusks, worms, and crustaceans. Their well-developed teeth even allow the larger members of the family to crack open small sea urchins.

Some wrasses feed upon the parasites of other fishes; *Labroides dimidiatus*, which is also the species most familiar to aquarists, dines exclusively upon such fare. At a fixed spot, they await the arrival of fish that present their flanks, opercula, gills, and mouths for inspection without showing any fear of predation. This characteristic cleaning behavior is also practiced by juvenile specimens of several species of *Bodianus*, *Halichoeres*, and *Thalassoma*, but disappears as they near adulthood.

A few wrasses of the genera *Labrus* and *Crenilabrus* spawn in a nest constructed in the sand or in a stand of algae, and defend their eggs and fry. The eggs typically hatch in four to five days. Other wrasses spawn in midwater. Buoyed by a drop of oil, the eggs rise to the surface where they are swept away by the prevailing current. The larvae of these species hatch a day or two later.

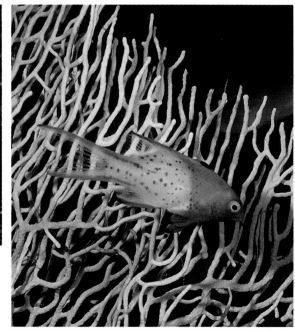

▲ *The twinspot hogfish (Bodianus bimaculatus) grows only 4 in (10 cm) long. Despite its small size, it is a quarrelsome fish whose tankmates must be chosen carefully.*

▶ *A juvenile lyretailed hogfish (Bodianus anthioides). Adults are less intensely colored.*

◀ These hues are distributed differently in male and female flame wrasses (Cirrhilabrus jordani), but the color pattern of both sexes is a blend of yellow, bright orange, and red.

▶ The sole species of its genus, the cigar wrasse (Chelio inemis) lives in beds of eelgrass. A bright lemon-yellow color form of this species also exists.

▲ The blue-sided pygmy wrasse (Cirrhilabrus cyanopleura) lives in harems.

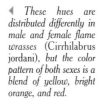

▲ The Ryuku pygmy wrasse (Cirrhilabrus ryukyuiensis) feeds on small planktonic organisms it picks from the water column in the vicinity of soft coral colonies.

◀ Juvenile clown wrasses (Coris aygula, also known as Coris angulata), are as attractively colored as adult fish are drab. As they grow progressively larger, gray is replaced by a faded blue. This species grows over 3 ft (1 m) long.

▲ Better known by its synonym, Coris formosa, the queen wrasse (Coris frerei) must be kept over a nonabrasive substratum, as it loves to bury itself at night.

The Story of Spots

Juvenile phase bicolor hogfish (B o d i a n u s mesothorax, shown at left) and spotfin hogfish (Bodianus axillaris) are virtually identical in appearance, with their large light spots on a dusky background. One way of avoiding confusion: Young bicolor hogfish have more spots on their back than on their belly and are somewhat yellower.

▲ The female color phase of the bird wrasse (Gomphosus varius). Males are blue-green in color.

▲ Closely related to Cirrhilabrus, the fairy wrasses of the genus Paracheilinus can be distinguished by the elegant elongations of their dorsal fin rays.

▲ This black-spot canary wrasse (Halicoeres leucoxanthus), barely 4 in (10 cm) long, is a dwarf of the genus.

▶ The harlequin tuskfish (Choerodon fasciatus) is one of the most sought-after wrasse species. Its color pattern remains almost the same throughout its life. This species is better known under the name Lienardella fasciata.

▼ One of the wrasses most commonly kept as an aquarium fish, the common cleaner (Labroides dimidiatus).

Wrasses (continued)

Wrasses are strictly diurnal fish. To spend their nights in peace, some species bury themselves in the sand; others nestle under a rock or a coral head. Still others find a hiding place and secrete a cocoon of protective mucus that isolates them from potential predators.

Most wrasses make good aquarium fish. They should be housed in a large tank furnished with a thick layer of fine sand, which they will use as a bed, and fed a varied diet, based on the flesh of mussels and shrimp with occasional algae or soft-leafed aquatic vegetation. To introduce most large wrasses and even a few of the smaller species to a tank containing live corals and tubeworms is to run the risk of seeing its invertebrate fauna decimated. As long as you research their dietary preferences carefully, there is no reason why many small wrasses cannot coexist happily with a wide range of invertebrates.

▲ The vermiculated dragon wrasse (Macropharyngodon bipartitus) lives in harems. Shown here is the female color phase.

▼ Closely related to the checkered wrasse (Halichoeres hortulanus), Halichoeres centiquadrus differs in lacking a second yellow spot beneath the dorsal fin.

▲ The impressive canine teeth of the red-breasted wrasse (Cheilinus fasciatus) speak volumes about its feeding pattern. This carnivorous species is particularly fond of large invertebrates.

◀ A canary wrasse (Halichoeres chrysus) in the company of a bun star (Culcita sp.).

Wrasse and Wrasse

This photo shows how much diversity can be found within a single family of fish. A common cleaner wrass is removing ecto-parasites from a Napoleon wrasse. The former measures 4 in (10 cm) long, the latter is a 7-ft-long (2.3 m) giant. Although it never grows this large in captivity, the Napoleon wrasse is suitable only as a subject for public aquaria. With its nuchal hump in the shape of a Phrygian cap and its mobile eyes, it is a most impressive fish. Divers in search of this species rarely find it, but it will sneak up behind them while they are undergoing decompression stops. Easily "tamed" with the help of such treats as hard-boiled eggs, it can become the target of spear fishermen in search of an impressive trophy. Happily, if the skin of its scaleless head is soft as velvet, the flanks are armored with scales tough enough to deflect a spear. In Polynesia, young fish under 20 in (50 cm) are greatly appreciated for their savory flesh, while that of two out of every three large adults, known locally as "mara," is poisonous.

▲ The stippled wrasse (Macropharyngodon geoffroyi) feeds on mollusks, which it removes from their shells with the help of its prominent lips and canine teeth.

▼ The subadult color phase of the checkered wrasse (Halichoeres hortulanus).

▲ Choat's wrasse (Macropharyngodon choati) is one of the easiest species of the genus to maintain in captivity.

▲ Despite its beauty, this fish (Stetojulis bandanensis) is not a good candidate for life in captivity. No species of the genus lives longer than a few months in an aquarium.

◀ A Red Sea endemic, Klunzinger's wrasse (Thalassoma klunzingeri) lives in relatively shallow water.

▼ After seeing this terminal phase male, it is hard to believe that initial phase male and female bluehead wrasses (Thalassoma bifasciatum) are lemon yellow in color.

▲ The saddleback wrasse (Thalassoma duperreyi) is extremely abundant in Hawaiian waters. As with all Thalassoma species, water of extremely high quality is essential to its successful maintenance.

▼ The six-lined wrasse (Pseudocheilinus hexatae-nia) can be recommended without reservation to novice marine aquarists.

▲ In nature, initial phase males of the Cortez rainbow wrasse (Thalassoma luca-sanum) are group spawners, whereas older terminal phase males are pair spawners.

▲ Its lyre-shaped caudal fin sets the red swallowtail grouper (Variola louti) apart from the red argus grouper (Cephalopholis miniata). It can grow to 30 in (80 cm) in nature.

▶ A common fish in the Red Sea and the remainder of the Indo-Pacific region, the red argus grouper seldom strays far from its cave. It adapts well to captivity.

Groupers and Their Relatives

Those who dive the reefs of the Red Sea or the Maldives are invariably impressed by their swarms of small—2- to 4-in-long (5 to 10 cm)—orange fish, which go by the name of sea goldfish or coral perch. They are representatives of the large Family Serrandiae, which also includes groupers that can attain a length of 8 ft (2.4 m) and a weight in excess of 600 lbs (272 kg). The Serranidae comprise over 400 species grouped into 76 genera. The family has been divided into five subfamilies.

Coral perches are tightly bound to the reef. It is unusual for them to rise more than 1 ft (30 cm) above the tallest coral head to snap up the zooplankton that constitutes their principal food source. At the least alarm, the entire swarm retreats to the shelter of the reef's branching corals. Above the same patch of coral, a single male keeps watch over his harem of females. If he should disappear, within a few days the dominant female of the group will change into a male and assume his role.

Like their temperate zone cousins, tropical groupers first mature as females, becoming males as they grow older; such fish are referred to as protogynous hermaphrodites. Groupers can live for 50 years and occupy the same cave for decades. They are thus easy targets for spear fishermen, and grouper populations worldwide are in decline.

Some groupers can rapidly change color to match their background. It is not inappropriate to describe this process as mimicry.

Other species become redder at greater depths. All groupers are ambush predators that await the approach of prey. It is very rare to see a grouper hunting out in the open.

Only the smallest serranids are suitable home aquarium residents, although large groupers are often the stars of public aquaria. Coral perch are the most easily maintained members of the family. A number of specimens will live amicably in a 75- to 100-gal (300 to 400 L) reef aquarium. These fish are midwater spawners so the chances of breeding them successfully are slight unless one can find some way to capture the eggs before they are lost.

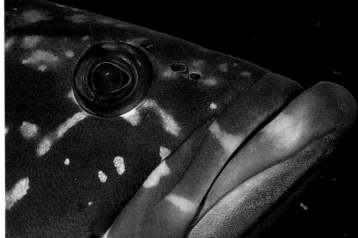

▲ The male purple queen (Pseudanthias tuka), shown here, is less brightly colored than the female. In this case, the female is the more attractive of the two sexes.

▶ The blue-striped grouper (Cephalopholis boenack) is easily maintained in a large aquarium. It readily accepts offerings of nonliving food.

▼ The lory anthias (Pseudanthias lori) is a diminutive marvel only rarely offered for sale. Surprisingly, this specimen has decided to hunt in the open.

▶ The male phase of the square spot coral perch (Pseudanthias pleurotaenia).

◀ The orange coral perch (Pseudanthias squamipinnis) is the first fish that a diver encounters in the shallows, always closely associated with coral colonies.

▶ As is the case in many species of coral perch, the female Pseudanthias pleurotaenia, shown here, is less brightly colored than the male.

Grace Kelly

Formerly and still widely known as the panther grouper, Chromileptes altivelis was renamed the "Grace Kelly grouper" in 1960. Aquarium specimens may reach 16 in (40 cm). Juveniles sport a pattern of large black polka dots on a white background. As they grow larger, the white becomes "dirtier," developing a beige, grayish, or faintly reddish cast. The number of spots multiplies as they decrease in size. This species should not be housed with smaller tankmates, which they are likely to treat as live food. They should be offered a choice of potential shelters and must not be housed with boisterous tankmates.

▲ Easily recognized thanks to its combination of blue spots and lighter bars, this peacock grouper (Cephalopholis argus) patrols a Polynesian reef.

▲ Attractive color pattern and appealing face notwithstanding, taking home a juvenile potato grouper (Epinephelus tukula) is not a good idea—this species grows 6 ft (2 m) long in nature.

▲ A common Florida resident, the lantern bass (Serranus baldwini) is an ideal choice for a mid-sized aquarium. This species grows about 4 in (10 cm) long.

▶ The white-spotted grouper (Epinephelus multinotatus) can change its color pattern to match that of its prey in order to approach it more easily.

▼ The color pattern of the shy hamlet (Hypoplectrus unicolor guttavarius) is quite different from that of the other hamlets.

▲ There is really only a single species of hamlet (Hypoplectrus unicolor), which exists in 10 recognized color forms. Shown here is a blue hamlet, Hypoplectrus unicolor gemma.

▼ The coloration of this fish is intermediate between that of the shy hamlet and the yellow-breasted hamlet (Hypoplectrus unicolor abberrans).

▲ *A juvenile clown triggerfish* (Balistoides conspicillum), *the favorite triggerfish of marine fish fanciers.*

▶ *Like the other members of the family, the queen triggerfish* (Balistes vetula) *is very partial to sea urchins. It squirts a stream of water at an urchin to knock it over, then attacks its unprotected underside, literally tearing it apart.*

▲ *Sea grass beds as well as coral reefs are the domain of the warty triggerfish* (Rhinecanthus verrucosus).

▼ *In nature, the Red Sea triggerfish* (Rhinecanthus assasi) *immobilizes its prey by first biting out their eyes.*

▼ *As the Picasso triggerfish* (Rhinecanthus aculeatus) *grows only 8 in (20 cm) long in captivity, one could envisage keeping a compatible couple in a large aquarium.*

Triggerfish

The eyes of triggerfish, like those of chameleons, are capable of independent movement and speak volumes about this fish's behavior! Triggers are among the most heavily armed of all fish. Brightly colored, their highly mobile eyes are placed high up on their heads, affording them an extremely wide field of vision. Their ventral fins have been replaced by a single stout spine, which they can erect at will. A clever modification of its first three spines allows this fish to lock the dorsal fin in an upright position. When these two spines are erected simultaneously, a triggerfish confronts a potential adversary with an unassailably bony triangle. If this does not suffice to put him to flight, he runs the risk of receiving a blow from a powerful tail well armed with sharp projections. Also, triggerfish threaten their enemies with cracking sounds. These are very aggressive fish and divers have been known to be charged and even bitten by an irate triggerfish.

The juveniles of some triggerfish live in schools, but adults are solitary, wandering over the sandy zones adjacent to coral reefs. Triggerfish spend the night jammed into crevices.

With their powerful dentition, triggerfish can easily crack the armor of crustaceans and successfully attack sea urchins, sea stars, and even stony corals. However, triggerfish enjoy a varied diet, consuming algae, sponges, and even attacking weak or injured fish. Obviously, it is impossible to keep more than a single specimen per tank in even the largest aquaria.

These fish are very hardy, easily acclimated to aquarium life, and quite capable of many years in captivity. The spawning behavior of one of the most commonly imported species, the Picasso triggerfish (*Rhinecanthus aculeatus*) has been observed in public aquaria.

▲ *Superbly colored but extremely aggressive, the wavy triggerfish* (Balistapus undulatus) *must be kept by itself. Even a very large tank provides no guarantee of safety to its other residents.*

▲ A school of black triggerfish (Melichthys niger) soliciting a handout from divers in Polynesia.

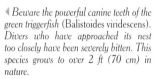

▲ The Indian triggerfish (Melichthys indicus), shown above, can be distinguished from the black triggerfish by the dark streak across its cheek.

◀ Beware the powerful canine teeth of the green triggerfish (Balistoides viridescens). Divers who have approached its nest too closely have been severely bitten. This species grows to over 2 ft (70 cm) in nature.

▲ The color pattern of the speckled triggerfish (Pseudobalistes flavimarginatus) is not very attractive. This fish is often eaten in Polynesia.

▲ The whiteline triggerfish bears the Latin name Sufflamen bursa. Bursa means purse. Seamen formerly used the cured skin of this fish to manufacture purses.

▲ Like the majority of triggerfish, the dusky triggerfish (Pseudobalistes fuscus) is easily maintained but extremely intolerant of tankmates of its own family.

▶ Blue, yellow, green, pink, the red-tailed triggerfish (Melichthys vidua) has complementary but surprisingly unexpected hues.

▼ The coloration of its caudal fin has earned Sufflamen chrysopterus the common name of double-tailed triggerfish.

▲ Midnight triggerfish (Odonus niger) live over reef slopes. Although occasional spawnings have been observed in the aquarium, these remain isolated episodes. Attempts to rear the resulting fry ended in failure.

▶ A close-up view of the caudal peduncle of the wavy triggerfish (Balistapus undulatus). The scales concealed in the black spot are modified to form forward-pointing curved hooks that constitute a formidable weapon. Great care must be taken when handling this fish in captivity.

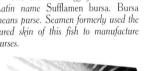

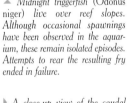

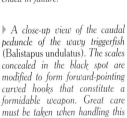

▼ The counter-striped triggerfish (Xanthichthys mento).

From Cardinalfish to Sharks

▲ *Its debonair appearance notwithstanding, the long-nosed hawkfish (Oxycirrhites typus) is a formidable predator of small invertebrates. This is the hawkfish of choice for the reef aquarium.*

The cardinalfish of the Family Apogonidae inhabit coral reefs and the waters of their associated lagoons. Most of the family's 200-odd species grow no larger than 4 in (10 cm) and are essentially nocturnal in their behavior, as is evident from their outsized eyes. Mouthbrooding appears to be the norm. The male appears to be the ovigerous parent, although contradictory reports have been received about which sex carries the eggs in the Bangaii cardinalfish. The hawkfish of the Family Cirrhitidae live on the same floor as the cardinalfish; they spend much of their time resting on a raised perch. Like cardinalfish, hawkfish are ideal candidates for a midsized aquarium. Sporting attractive juvenile coloration, which makes them highly saleable, these fish quickly grow to an awkwardly large size. Snappers and sweetlips, for example, while quite cute at a length of 4 in (10 cm) grow to an adult size of 2 to 3 ft (60 to 90 cm) long.

The difficulties of acclimating many other species to captivity have proven insurmountable. These fish never live more than a few weeks in the aquarium.

The importation of such fish is often environmentally destructive. Although such practices are dying out, some marine tropicals are still captured using inhumane collecting techniques. In both Indonesia and the Philippines, potassium cyanide is still used in the reef environment to "anesthetize" fish and make them easier to catch. The reef recovers poorly from such repeated doses of cyanide; fish so immobilized are afflicted with liver and kidney lesions from which they never recover. The marine aquarium hobby can advance only when the public is well informed.

◀ *The coral reef is home to many different species of hawkfish. They can be found over a depth range of 3 to 120 ft (91 to 305 cm). Here, the 3-in-long (7 cm) dwarf hawkfish (Cirrhichthys falco).*

▶ *An ideal choice for a large aquarium, the threadfin snapper (Symphorichthys spilurus) is a hardy and peaceful fish.*

▼ *The superb golden color form of Parupeneus cyclostomus, the lemon goatfish, photographed on the coral reefs of the Red Sea. These fish are easily maintained but do best when kept in small groups of five to seven individuals.*

▲ *Often confused with the big-eyed cardinalfish (Sphaeramia orbicularis), the pyjama cardinalfish (Sphaeramia nematoptera) has a more brightly colored head; its eyes are bright red.*

▼ *Since its debut as an aquarium fish in 1996, the Bangaii cardinalfish (Pterapogon kauderni) quickly stole the limelight from the pyjama cardinalfish. Furthermore, it breeds readily in captivity (shown here is an ovigerous male) and the fry are easily reared.*

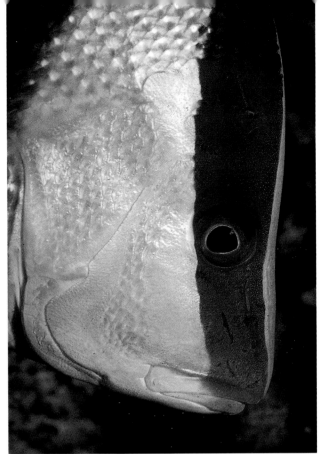

▲ In nature, groups of royal grammas (Gramma loreto) live in caves. Such an arrangement can be duplicated only in the very largest of home aquaria. Failing this, one must make do with a solitary specimen.

◄ The emperor snapper (Lujanus sebae) is only suitable for public aquaria; it grows over 3 ft (90 cm) long. It is an important food fish throughout the Indo-Pacific region.

▼ This black-banded juvenile golden trevally (Gnatha-nodon speciosus) seeks out the shelter afforded by a long-finned batfish (Platax teira).

▼ The striped sweetlips (Plectorhynchus orientalis) uses its soft, thick lips to dislodge worms and mollusks buried in the mud.

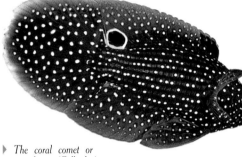

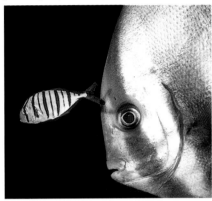

► The coral comet or marine betta (Calloplesiops altivelis). It is difficult for a potential predator to find the fish's head.

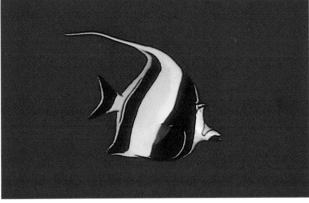

▲ The Moorish idol (Zanclus cornutus) does not adapt well to life in captivity. Amazingly, these fish can be found in seaports and other polluted habitats in the Indo-Pacific region.

▼ In captivity as in nature, the common bigeye (Priacanthus hamrur) needs access to dark caves to feel fully at ease.

▼ While not recommended for the amateur aquarist, many sharks, like this woebegong (Orectolobus ornatus) can be successfully maintained by public aquariums.

▼ Like the different wobegongs, the nurse shark (Ginglymostoma cirratum) spends most of its time on the bottom in the shelter of a rocky overhang.

◄ While adult porkfish live in large schools over rocky bottoms and in the vicinity of reefs, and feed on zooplankton and benthic invertebrates, juveniles are cleaner fish, removing ectoparasites from other fish. Here a juvenile porkfish (Anisotremus virginicus), which ranges from Florida southward to Brazil, cleans the fins of a nurse shark.

Sharks and Aquariums

Divers are familiar with the blacktip reef shark (Carcharhinus melanopterus), a common inhabitant of reefs and tropical lagoons. This is the "pelagic" shark most often displayed by public aquaria. The management of such institutions, driven by the public's demand for the sensational, find themselves in competition to refine their husbandry techniques while constructing progressively larger display tanks. Who can complain about this trend? Certainly not the visitor, nor the sharks themselves, now able to cruise through progressively larger volumes of water. In Japan, a whale shark (Rhincodon typus), the largest living fish, is now being maintained in captivity, where it daily consumes bushels of plankton.

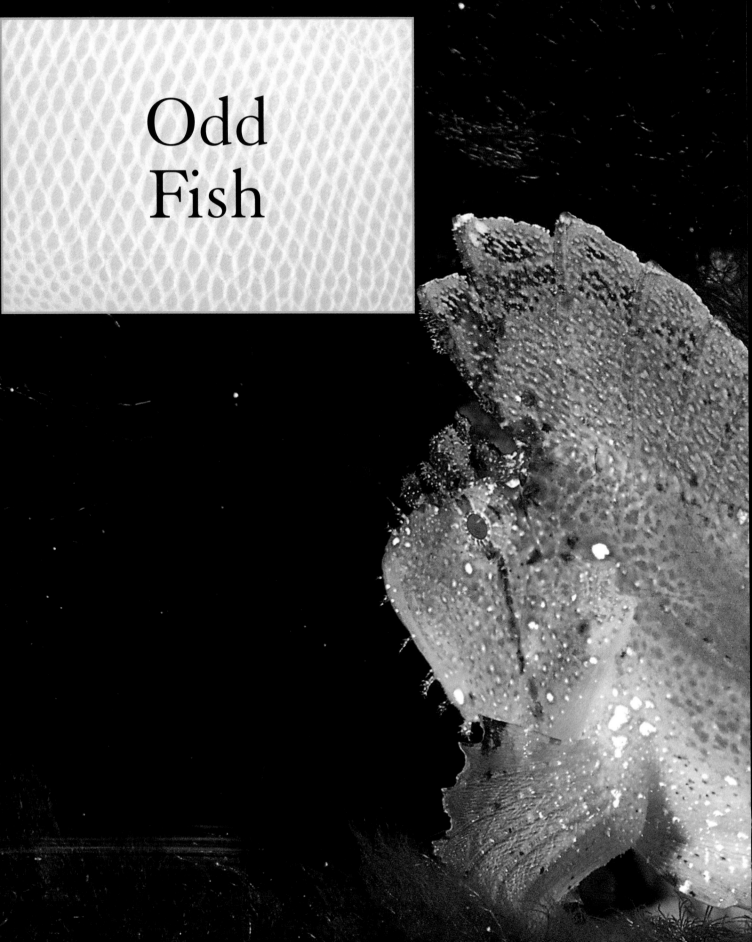

Odd
Fish

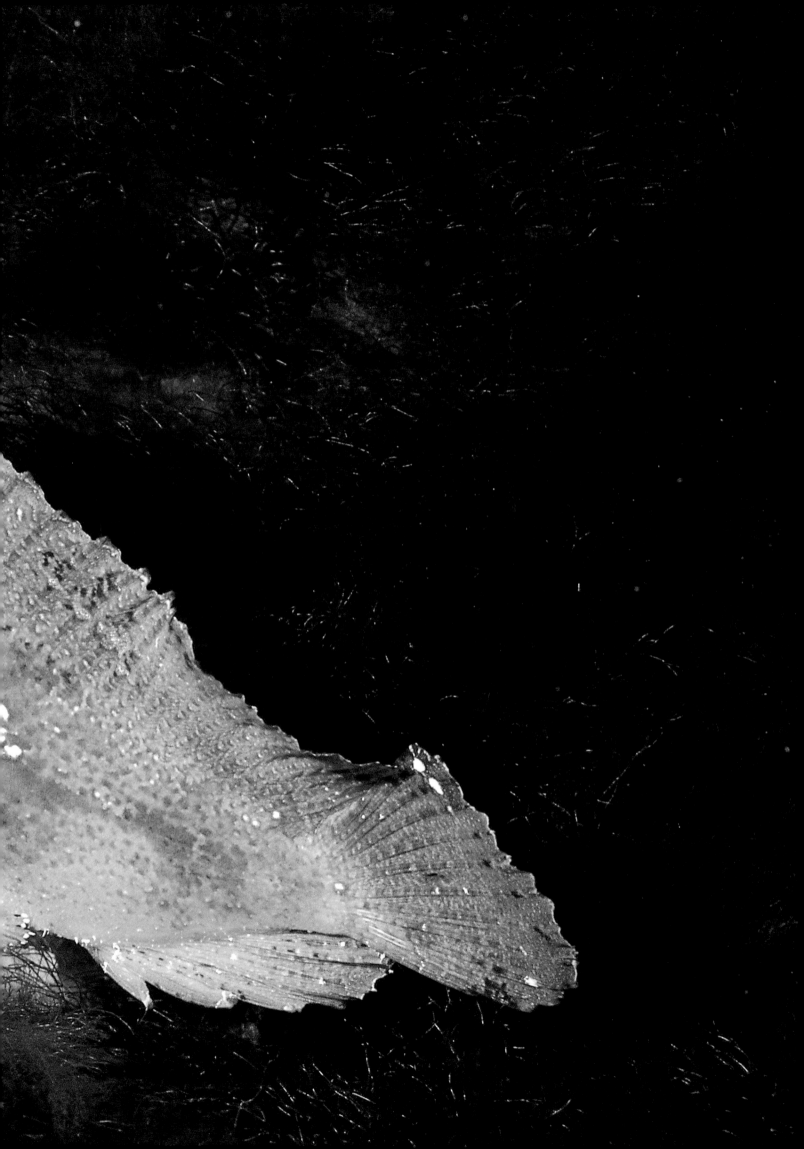

▲ A young mottled lionfish (Pterois miles) on the hunt over a Red Sea reef.

▲ The two horizontal white lines on the caudal peduncle of the white-rayed lionfish (Pterois radiata) differentiate it from its congeners.

▼ Close-up view of the venomous dorsal spines of the common lionfish (Pterois volitans).

Scorpions and Frogs

The Suborder Scorpaenoidei comprises seven families—more, according to some systems of classification. The group includes among their number the celebrated lionfish and stonefish.

In tropical countries, these fish are believed to constitute a real threat to swimmers and recreational divers, while closer to home, they are thought to pose a danger to city-dwelling aquarists. The lionfish of the genera Pterois and Dendrochirus are essentially nocturnal reef dwellers, although one sometimes finds small groups foraging in the daytime. Thanks to an enormous mouth, these fish can swallow prey as large as themselves. Despite their modest size—between 4 and 14 in (10 to 35 cm) in overall length—lionfish have few predators, largely because they possess a battery of venomous dorsal spines. In the aquarium, scorpionfish should be kept only with companions their own size or larger. As they may be dominated by more active tankmates at feeding time, it is a good idea to feed each specimen individually. Each lionfish should be given 25 to 30 gal (100 to 150 L) worth of living space over and above the needs of the other species with which it shares quarters.

Although quite unsuitable for home aquaria, stonefish are frequently exhibited in public aquaria. These fish possess the same sort of venomous spines as do scorpionfish. Sitting in ambush between rocks and clumps of algae in the shallows of estuaries or coastal reefs, depending on the species in question, these fish are effectively invisible and therefore, potentially very dangerous. The glands at the base of their dorsal spines produce a venom particularly toxic to mammals that can prove lethal to humans. This weaponry is entirely defensive, as stonefish have no way of actively attacking an enemy.

Indeed, pressure on the dorsal spines inflicts the wounds by which the stonefish's venom enters the body.

Members of the Family Antennariidae, frogfish are relatives of anglerfish. They are noteworthy for the fact that they literally "fish" for their meals. A hobbyist ignorant of their behavior who wishes to house two specimens of the same size together runs the risk of seeing one swallow the other. These fish are reef dwellers and sport magnificent coloration that varies as a function of their habitat.

▲ The antenna lionfish (Pterois antennata) enjoys a wide geographic distribution.

▶ The Hawaiian lionfish lives at a greater depth—to 400 ft (120 m)—than any other species of the genus.

◀ The disproportionately long fin rays of the common lionfish give a certain elegance to this fish.

▲ *The flaps around the mouth of this leafy scorpionfish (Rhinopias frondosa) predict its gluttonous appetite.*

▶ *Rhinopias such as this unidentified species live among stands of algae, where they are effectively undetectable.*

◀ *Portrait shot of a painted anglerfish (Antennarius pictus), its lure at rest.*

Fishing Party

The anglerfish brandishes the lure located on top of its head, a structure whose shape is unique to each species. The shape of the lure corresponds to that of the intended victim's preferred food source. When the victim approaches, the anglerfish opens its mouth so rapidly that the prey is swept inside by the current of water. The lure is at the end of a specialized rodlike structure derived from a highly modified dorsal fin spine. The hunting behavior of this Antennarius hispidus persists even in the aquarium.

▼ *The Mollucas anglerfish (Antennarius moluccensis) exists in several distinct and variable color forms.*

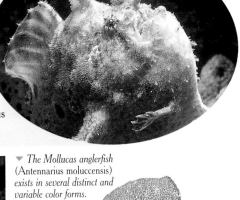

▲ *It is difficult to make out the true shape of the giant anglerfish (Antennarius commersonii) in this amorphous heap.*

▼ *This cockatoo leaffish (Ablabys taenianotus) allows itself to sway back and forth with the current, like a strand of algae. Prey are easily trapped.*

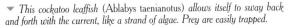

▲ *Were it not caught by a photoflash, this tufted scorpionfish (Scorpaenopsis oxycephala) would go undetected in the midst of these rocks.*

▼ *This demonic scorpionfish (Scorpaenopsis diabolus) is resting on a detritus-covered bottom.*

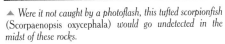

◀ *The sometimes lethal venom of the stonefish (Synanceia verrucosa), whose eye is visible in the adjacent photo, is sometimes collected for medical purposes.*

▲ *Flaps of skin and scales modified to form thorny projections are the assets of the ragged scorpionfish (Scorpaenopsis venosa).*

▲ *The saddleback sharp-nosed puffer (Canthigaster valentini) can be differentiated from its close relative, the crowned sharp-nosed puffer (Canthigaster coronata) by the fact that its two lateral "saddles" extend to the venter.*

▶ *Pronounced sexual dimorphism makes it a simple matter to distinguish between male (shown here) and female ornate boxfish (Aracana ornata). The latter are a uniform brown marked with fine white streaks.*

▲ *Cowfish (Lactoria cornuta) up to 30 in (80 cm) long have been collected in Polynesia. The caudal fin of this species can be as long as its body.*

▼ *The splendid color pattern of the male polka-dot boxfish (Ostracion meleagris). Females are marked with white spots on a chocolate brown background.*

Balloons, Trunks, and Porcupines

Grouped under this Pythonesque heading are the very unusual fishes of the Order Tetraodontiformes—literally, the four-toothed fish. With their teeth fused into a stout beak, puffers, sometimes known as blowfish, can successfully overcome a wide range of prey inaccessible to less well endowed predators. Their flesh is greatly esteemed in Asia, especially Japan, no doubt for its flavor. A taste for danger also enters into this equation, for *fugu*, as these fish are called in Japanese, concentrate tetradontoxin in several internal organs, a poison far more toxic than cyanide. Puffers can be found in the world's tropical and temperate seas and a number of species routinely enter brackish water. When threatened, puffers swallow a lot of water. By thus inflating themselves, they quickly stop any predatory notions an aggressor might have.

Trunkfish belong to two different families, the Aracanidae and the Ostraciidae. They are characterized by solid bodies covered with armor made up of fused scale plates, making them largely immune to predators. They typically live on coral reefs, where they feed on crustaceans and echinoderms.

The porcupine fish of the Family Diodontidae superficially resemble puffers; they can also change their shape by swallowing water. Covered with spines that they erect when inflating themselves, they are generally avoided by predators, but young porcupine fish living in open water are preferred food items of large pelagic species such as tuna and marlin.

Easily acclimated to life in captivity, these fish make satisfactory aquarium residents provided they are restricted to a tank with tankmates that have similar maintenance requirements. Many of them grow quite large and their dietary preferences often prevent plans to decorate their quarters as live invertebrates are clearly out of the question. Also, several species of boxfish release a toxin into the water when stressed that is apt to prove lethal to their tankmates as well as themselves. Handle these fish with extreme care.

◀ *Sharp-nosed puffers feed on algae and sessile invertebrates. They should not be added to a tank of live corals. Shown here, the spotted sharp-nosed puffer (Canthigaster solandri).*

▶ *The barred porcupine fish (Diodon holacanthus) is the Diodon species most widely kept as an aquarium fish.*

▲ The yellow color phase of the spotted dog-faced puffer (Arothron nigropunctatus).

▲ Close-up view of the formidable dentition of the speckled dog-faced puffer (Arothron hispidus). Take care when handling these fish!

▲ The scribbled dog-faced puffer (Arothron mappa) never moves far from its shelter. Photographed in the Maldives.

◄ Puffers have always appealed to aquarists because of their interesting faces. Here, the spotted dog-faced puffer (Arothron nigropunctatus).

▲ Easily recognizable thanks to its black half-mask, the masked dog-faced puffer (Arothron diadematus) is endemic to the Red Sea.

▶ The yellow color phase of the polka-dot dog-faced puffer (Arothron meleagris) closely resembles that of Arothron nigropunctatus. This species can still be encountered in the literature as Arothron citrinellus.

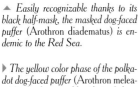

▼ The polka-dot dog-faced puffer (Arothron meleagris) in its highly characteristic and more easily recognizable white-spotted color form.

▲ The spotted porcupine fish (Diodon hystrix) is often confused with the barred porcupine fish; however, it grows to nearly 3 ft (90 cm).

◄ That is what becomes of porcupine fish in the tourist shops of many tropical countries.

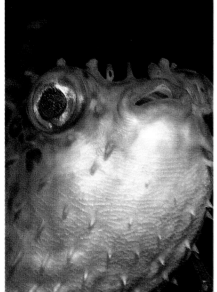

◄ Large eyes and a body covered with sharp spines set porcupine fish apart from puffers. Shown here a yellow-spotted porcupine fish (Cyclichthys spilostylus).

The Porcupine Fish Inflated

Face-to-face encounters between divers and porcupine fish are quite impressive when the latter inflates itself to discourage a potential enemy. These fish prefer flight to inflation; once an individual is fully inflated, swimming becomes impossible. It is best to avoid eliciting this defensive response and, when moving a porcupine fish between tanks, do not ever allow it to inflate itself with air. Shown here, an ocellated porcupine fish (Diodon liturosus), photographed in the Seychelles.

▲ *This young starry moray (Echidna nebulosa) has taken shelter in a dead coral skeleton.*

▶ *Moray eels often live as pairs, the two partners sharing the same cave. The appearance of these yellow-jawed moray eels (Gymnothorax nudivomer), photographed in the Red Sea, betrays their specific identity.*

Ribbons and Needles

▲ *The Java moray eel (Gymnothorax javanicus) reaches nearly 10 ft (3 m). It is not uncommon to surprise a pair in the course of an amorous frolic, as here on Australia's Great Barrier Reef.*

▼ *The yellow-spotted moray eel (Muraena lentiginosa).*

▲ *The zebra moray eel (Echidna zebra) adjusts readily to captivity. It can grow almost 5 ft (1.5 m) long.*

▼ *The spotted moray eel (Gymnothorax moringa) of the Antilles has been observed at a depth of 650 ft (200 m).*

▲ *An ideal subject for a "small" aquarium, the streaked-fin moray eel (Gymnothorax zonipectis) grows no longer than 18 in (45 cm).*

Sea needles, members of the Family Syngnathidae, and moray eels are often compared to colored ribbons.

The Family Muraenidae comprises over 200 species grouped into 15 genera. They range in size from 8 in (20 cm) to over 12 ft (3.7 m) long. Morays have a reputation for being aggressive, as evidenced by the number of people who have been badly bitten, but much of this "aggressiveness" stems from the fact that morays are very nearsighted so a tendency to confuse a diver's fingers with the tentacles of a succulent octopus can be excused. Morays spend much of their lives in the shelter of the reef's crannies and crevices, with only their heads protruding. Their gaping jaws, which must remain open if they are to breathe, give morays a terrifying appearance. These eels leave their refuges only when hunting for food. The large, rearward-pointing teeth of many species leave no doubt as to their essentially carnivorous feeding pattern. Only the smallest moray eels can be kept successfully in the home aquarium. The larger moral eels can be successfully housed only in the large display tanks of a public aquarium.

Sea horses live in eelgrass beds and amid stands of algae, where they can find the minute crustaceans upon which they feed. The resemblance these fish bear to a horse has long been noted. Their reproductive pattern, first described by Aristotle, is among the most surprising to be encountered in the entire animal kingdom. The female deposits her eggs in a special pouch on the male's belly, where they are fertilized. The male retains the developing eggs until they are ready to hatch, at which point he uses the powerful contraction of his brood pouch's muscular walls to "deliver" the fry. In some pipefish, the brood pouch is replaced by a partially enclosed ventral brood chamber; in others, the female attaches the eggs to the male who carries them in his abdomen or between his ventral fins. Sea horses and their near relatives should be kept only with small, inoffensive tankmates.

▲ A moray eel should be individually fed during its initial period of acclimation. Shown here, a young black-eared moray eel (Muraena melanotis).

▼ The white-eyed moray eel (Sidera prosopeion), below, has a lilac-colored head and no dotted lines on the body.

Changing Ribbons

Bright blue and sooty black ribbon eels were formally described as different species. Later, it became evident that blue and black animals represented two distinct color phases of a single species, Rhinomuraena quaesita. Juvenile fish are black. They turn blue upon maturing as males. Under aquarium conditions, color reversals from blue to black have been observed. Females are bright yellow, having passed through an intermediate blue and yellow phase.

▲ A male pipefish (Syngnathoides sp.) giving birth to its young.

◀ Sea horses need thin, rigid supports, such as gorgonian skeletons, to wrap their prehensile tails around. They remain like this for hours, rocked by the currents of their aquarium.

▶ Many different species of sea horse, such as this magnificent golden individual, are imported. However, it is very difficult to identify them with any degree of accuracy. The fish shown in the adjacent photo could be Hippocampus kuda.

▲ A close-up view of the brood pouch and eggs of a "pregnant" male Syngnathoides.

▶ The yellow-banded pipefish (Corythoichthys flavofasciatus) searches through an algal mat for minute crustaceans.

▲ The male weedy sea dragon (Phyllopteryx taeniolatus) gives birth to young nearly 1 in (2.5 cm) long. Only young specimens adapt successfully to life in captivity.

▲ The zebra pipefish (Doryrhamphus dactyliophorus), like other syngnathids, requires live food of an appropriate size to prosper in captivity.

From Trumpets to Parrots

▲ *Hatpin urchins serve as a refuge for striped shrimpfish (Aeoliscus strigatus).*

▶ *Juvenile batfish resemble extraordinarily deep-bodied freshwater angelfish. Adults are almost perfectly circular in shape and lose their attractive color patterns. Shown here is a juvenile yellow fin batfish (Platax pinnatus).*

▲ *Close-up shot of a Napoleon wrasse (Cheilinus undulatus), showing its massive nuchal hump. This species must be observed either in nature or in a public aquarium.*

▶ *Often sold as an aquarium fish, the blue-spotted ray (Taeniura lymna) is easily tamed and will quickly learn to eat from its keeper's hand. Beware of the venomous barb located on the tail of this species, whether you encounter it while diving or while maintaining its tank. When disturbed, this ray can lash its tail like a whip, inflicting a painful wound to any limb that has the misfortune to disturb it.*

▶ *Despite the blue spots that are clearly visible when the fish is kept in an aquarium, this tropical flatfish (Bothus mancus) is undetectable on the sandy bottom of a tropical lagoon.*

◀ *The trumpetfish (Aulostomus maculatus) approaches its victims by letting itself be carried passively by the prevailing current, much like a piece of flotsam.*

▶ *The milky sole (Pardachirus marmoratus) secretes a bitter toxin from pores located at the base of its dorsal and anal fins. These toxins allow it to repel any predator that approaches it too closely.*

Some ocean harbor fish exploit their unusual shape to conceal themselves, as is the case with the trumpetfish, which hide behind a large herbivorous fish in order to sneak up on the smaller fish upon which it feeds. Shrimpfish live head down among the spines of hatpin urchins, where they can feed upon zooplankton without fear of being eaten themselves. Flat fish require specialized feeding adaptations. Rays have their mouths on their underside but their eyes are located on their dorsal surface. They thus feed blindly, foraging over sandy bottoms of lagoons and in the shallows adjacent to coral reefs. Other flat fish, such as soles, mimic their background with amazing accuracy, snapping up any "strollers" imprudent enough to approach them too closely.

Like the six known species of flashlight fish, the pinecone fish possesses two light-emitting organs, one beneath each eye. These organs are used as a means of communication by some species, but it is also possible that they are used to attract the small crustaceans upon which they feed, and may simply allow them to see more clearly. The filefish of the Family Monacanthidae have at various times been lumped with the triggerfishes, on the grounds that both groups possess an identical mechanism for locking the spiny dorsal fin erect. They differ from triggerfish in many aspects of their overall morphology and in their behavior. A number of filefish mimic the coloration of other species with great accuracy.

Tourists owe the white sand beaches on the shores of tropical islands to the parrotfish of the Family Scaridae. This travel poster image is largely due to the constant foraging of these fish, which crush the coral in order to dislodge the algae and minute invertebrates. The skeletons of hard corals are composed of indigestible calcium carbonate, which, once masticated by the fish, is expelled as a cloud of fine particles, contributing to the perpetuation of the popular image of a coral atoll.

▲ *The blue parrotfish (Scarus gibbus), here in its male phase, is endemic to the Red Sea.*

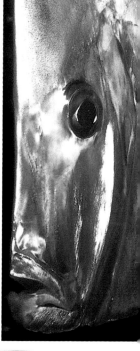

▲ *Adult male and female parrotfish of a given species are very differently colored. Shown here is the female phase of the blue parrotfish. Juveniles and subadults are colored identically regardless of their sex, although they may display different color patterns as they grow older. The coloration of many juvenile parrotfish is quite drab, ranging from beige to brown.*

▶ *Schools of lookdown (Selene vomser) can be found among the mangroves.*

◀ *The freckled filefish (Cantherines pullus) is usually found in shallow water, amid colonies of gorgonians.*

▲ *In addition to its attractive appearance, the leafy filefish (Chaetoderma penicilligera) is also hardy enough to be a good beginner's fish.*

▶ *Rather rare in nature, the white-spotted filefish (Cantherines macrocerus) is not often available to hobbyists.*

▼ *A tempting proposition because of its small size— no greater than 4 in (10 cm) long—and attractive color pattern, the orange-spotted filefish (Oxymonacanthus longirostris) should not be sold as an aquarium fish because of its specialized dietary requirements.*

Pocket Flashlight

The Australian pinecone fish (Cleidopus gloriamaris) possesses a photoluminescent organ on each jaw, situated immediately below the eye. The light is produced by luminescent bacteria. During the day, or under normal aquarium conditions, this organ is bright orange. At night, or at great depths, it glows pale green. The fish uses this light to hunt for minute crustaceans resting on the bottom. This species lives in water as deep as 500 ft (150 m). It can adapt to warmer water and can be kept successfully in an aquarium without using a chiller.

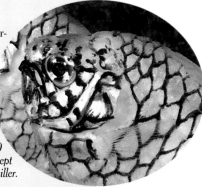

▼ *The scrawled filefish (Aluterus scriptus) is difficult to acclimate, despite the fact that it is unselectively omnivorous in nature.*

Indispensable Additions to a Freshwater Aquarium

▲ A knowledgeable aquarist will not be seduced by the brown-striped or clear lemon yellow shells of apple snails (shown here is Ampullaria australis). These snails will unfailingly devour any plant matter they come across. Even if generously fed with fresh lettuce and canned peas, they are quite prepared to attack even such tough-leafed aquatic plants as Anubias. Apple snails possess functional lungs and breathe through a long snorkel they direct upwards to the water surface.

▼ The Malaysian live-bearer (Melanoides tuberculata) is the indispensable aquarium snail. During the day, it burrows through the bottom, consuming particles of uneaten food and aerating the substratum, to the great benefit of growing plants. As it only emerges at night, its presence is unlikely to disturb those aquarists who find snails unattractive.

▲ Experience has shown that a freshwater aquarium comes into balance and aquatic plants grow best when about 80 percent of the tank bottom is planted. Here is a good example of such a tank, its plants free of encumbering algae and its residents at ease. The secret of success—plant heavily.

▶ Ramshorn snails are often accidentally introduced into a tank by means of plants carrying their clear, jelly-like egg masses. These snails are tireless con-sumers of algae and organic waste, up to and including dead fish. They only attack aquatic plants in poor condition.

▲ Anubias are the ideal plants for a novice aquarist's tank. Slow growing, they do not require constant pruning. Their tough leaves are ignored by most herbivorous fishes and serve as spawning sites for many different species. Anubias barteri has been used to recreate a Congo River biotope in this aquarium.

◀ Normally brown, the Moluc-cas sweeper prawn (Atya mol-uccensis) becomes bright orange immediately after molting. This specimen is carefully climbing out of its discarded exoskeleton. This species traps suspended food particles by incessantly waving its arms, which are covered with fine hairs, through the water.

▼ Once they have recovered from the birth process, young live-bearers hide in stands of aquatic plants to escape predation. This two-day-old swordtail is well protected among the leaves of this stand of umbrella grass (Eleocharis vivipara).

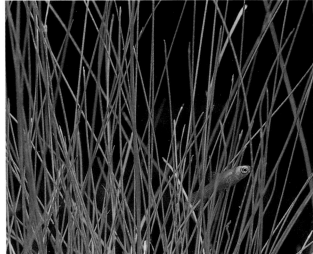

◀ Some fish deposit their eggs on brushy substrata, to which they cling by means of fine threads. They are thus held clear of the bottom and protected effectively against their many predators until they hatch. These tiger barbs are spawning in a bunch of cabomba (Cabomba caroliniana).

▶ Swordplants of the genus Echinodorus are for the most part suitable for only very large aquaria, although a few smaller species are commercially available. This large Amazon swordplant (Echinodorus sp.) is the preferred spawning site of a pair of angelfish. This plant, whose leaves can grow to a length of 18 in (50 cm), needs to be fertilized regularly in order to develop fully.

◀ Hornwort (Ceratophyllum demersum) is an indispensable source of shade for an aquarium housing shy fish that cannot endure bright light. It serves equally well as a spawning site and a refuge for fry, which often make their first meal of the microorganisms growing on its leaves.

▲ With its upright growth habit, the Java fern (Microsorum pteropus) is an imposing element in the decor of any aquarium. As it does not require a substratum—it should never be planted—it is an ideal plant for the small breeding tanks preferred by killifish enthusiasts.

◀ A spawning pair of lemon tetras dives into the thicket of pearlweed (Hemianthus micranthemoides), where they will deposit their eggs.

▼ Many aquatic plants are also cultivated as emergents. Illustrated here is the giant hygrophila (Hygrophila corymbosa). The leaves of plants grown out of water are so different in shape from those grown submerged that it may be difficult to recognize them as belonging to the same species. The shape of their flowers is the only absolutely reliable means of identification.

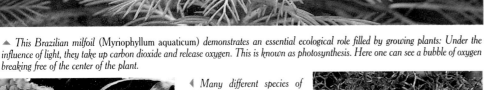

▲ This Brazilian milfoil (Myriophyllum aquaticum) demonstrates an essential ecological role filled by growing plants: Under the influence of light, they take up carbon dioxide and release oxygen. This is known as photosynthesis. Here one can see a bubble of oxygen breaking free of the center of the plant.

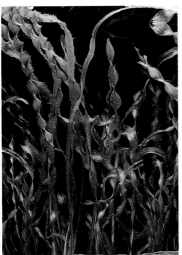

◀ Many different species of eelgrass are sold as aquarium plants, ranging in size from the giant Vallisneria, whose leaves can grow to a length of 7 ft (2 m) to "dwarf" species that reach a height of 18 to 30 in (50 to 80 cm). They are highly decorative, but their habit of reproducing asexually by means of runners makes them a rather invasive plant. The degree of regularity in the "twist" of these corkscrew vallisneria (Vallisneria americana var. biwaensis) plants is determined by both day length and light intensity.

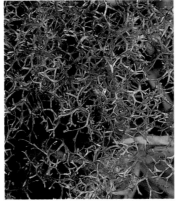

▶ Cultivating water lilies in the aquarium is possible if you assure their proper growth and possibly even induce flowering. Regular doses of fertilizer and careful pruning will determine whether they will produce floating leaves or a dense clump of smaller submerged leaves near the bottom. Shown here are the upper and lower surfaces of a floating leaf of the green lotus (Nymphaea lotus).

◀ Crystalwort (Riccia fluitans) is rarely offered for sale. Composed of many small intertwined forked stems, this aquatic liverwort floats at the water's surface, where it affords an excellent refuge to newly hatched fry. It requires very bright light for optimal growth.

▲ Mushroom anemones (Order Corallimorpharia) differ from true anemones in their internal structure. Because they are very hardy and are available in a wide range of shapes and colors, Discosoma species are very popular with marine hobbyists. As they reproduce asexually by budding from the base of an established individual or by symmetrical fission of individual polyps, colonies of mushroom anemones can spread very rapidly. Because they have a planktonic larval stage, successful sexual reproduction of these animals is unlikely in a filtered aquarium.

▲ Privileged hosts of clownfish in nature, anemones are essential adjuncts to any aquarium housing Amphiprion species. The Maldive clownfish (Amphiprion nigripes) is found only in association with a single species, the magnificent carpet anemone (Heteractis magnifica). Better known under its former designation of Radianthus ritteri, it is frequently offered for sale. Bear in mind that fully expanded, an individual can cover an area almost 4 ft (1.2 m) square. It clearly requires a large aquarium.

▼ Goniopora lobata, a hermatypic or stony coral, is highly sought after by advanced marine aquarists. It is difficult to understand how an organism that copes successfully with drying at low tide and lives in polluted waters in nature can prove so difficult to maintain in an apparently healthy aquarium. It appears that a certain type of algae is responsible for the deterioration of its skeleton in tanks with a high dissolved nitrate level. The polyps wilt and become flabby, the beginning of the end.

Indispensable Additions
to a Marine Aquarium

▲ There are over 1,000 species of sea anemone (Order Actinaria). These gelatinous animals, lacking any sort of rigid skeleton, are nonetheless formidable predators. Their tentacles are armed with nematocysts, specialized cells that discharge a type of miniature harpoon at the slightest touch. These harpoons deliver a powerful venom that paralyzes their prey. The tentacles of the bubble-tipped anemone (Entacmaea quadricolor) are not always as swollen as they appear to be in this photo. In nature, one can see either solitary specimens, such as this individual, photographed in the Red Sea, or in dense carpets comprising scores of individuals.

▲ Colonial anemones (Order Zoantharia) are an excellent beginner's choice, as they are relatively forgiving of a novice's mistakes. They will rapidly colonize any solid surface, be it rockwork or bivalve shells. Zoanthus species feed upon microplankton in nature, but in captivity, those species with a strong green cast can make do quite well with the nutrients provided by their algal symbiots, known as zooxanthellae. Here a Zoanthus praelargus spreads its colonies over an aquarium's rockwork.

▲ A marine aquarium devoted to European species, such as the Mediterranean tube anemone (Cerianthus membranaceus), is a perfectly feasible project. Elegant of form and vividly colored, it is the equal of any of its tropical cousins. These anemones must be kept over a rather deep substratum in order to properly anchor themselves to the bottom. Two types of tentacles extend outward from the protective tube, short oral tentacles that surround the mouth and much longer marginal tentacles, which the animal uses to capture its prey. This anemone requires a seasonal change in order to prosper in captivity.

▼ This is actually a sedentary worm that places its protective tube in the rocks or on the skeleton of hard corals such as Porites species. If the coral should die, the worm does not long survive it, although no one has been able to discover any vital connection between the two. The orange plumes that protrude from the tube on the right are modified gills of a Christmas tree tubeworm (Spirobranchus sp.). The tube on the left appears to be empty, but its resident worm withdrew its wreath after the first discharge of the flash used for this photo. Live rock and some coral colonies imported for the aquarium trade often conceal unexpected treasures. It is not unusual for them to support a number of Spirobranchus.

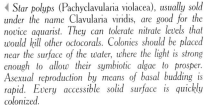

◀ *Star polyps* (Pachyclavularia violacea), *usually sold under the name* Clavularia viridis, *are good for the novice aquarist. They can tolerate nitrate levels that would kill other octocorals. Colonies should be placed near the surface of the water, where the light is strong enough to allow their symbiotic algae to prosper. Asexual reproduction by means of basal budding is rapid. Every accessible solid surface is quickly colonized.*

▶ *Soft corals of the genus* Dendronephthya *never cease to amaze divers, as here in the Red Sea but it is wiser to leave them in place rather than attempt to bring them back to one's aquarium, as they do not live long in captivity. The recent discovery of their dietary preferences—they feed on phytoplankton—should lead to further efforts to maintain them. These animals are swollen with water and owe their rigidity to the fine calcareous spicules that also give them their bright colors.*

▼ *Numerous small inhalant orifices draw water containing dissolved oxygen and food to the colony's component cells, while a smaller number of large exhalant orifices carry away spent water and metabolic wastes. While some tubular or bushy sponges contribute to a tank's decor, others, such as the red boring sponge (*Cliona vastifica*) should be eliminated if it appears in a shipment of live rock. Its ability to dissolve calcareous substrates makes it a veritable plague; be warned that a number of aquarium fish enthusiastically devour sponges.*

▶ *The beauty of cowries, with their shiny shells and delicately patterned mantles has won them many admirers. The tiger cowry (*Cypraea tigris*) is a favorite of aquarists. This animal is nocturnal and one must be aware of its potential to do damage. Its powerful foot may very well dislodge painstakingly positioned invertebrate colonies. Though a herbivore, not all corals are spared its attentions.*

◀ *Hermit crabs are hardy aquarium residents that should only be added to a tank devoid of other kinds of invertebrates. About 80 species of hermit crabs, all more or less brightly colored, are known. With each molt, they grow progressively larger and must be furnished a selection of larger empty shells. Shell-swapping by these unarmored but very "hairy" crustaceans is a sight worth seeing. Shown here is the red reef hermit (*Dardanus megistos*).*

▲ *Some giant clams can grow to a width of nearly 5 ft (1.5 m), while others never grow larger than 6 in (15 cm). It is not easy to distinguish between the two or three species usually sold in the aquarium trade. Their only husbandry requirements are perfect water quality and a moderate amount of current. The nutritional needs of giant clams are satisfied by their zooxanthellae, which also account for the vivid coloration of their mantles. These different color patterns are of little use in the identification of different species—the key diagnostic characteristic is rather the morphology of the shell.*

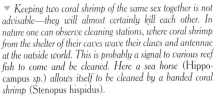

▼ *Keeping two coral shrimp of the same sex together is not advisable—they will almost certainly kill each other. In nature one can observe cleaning stations, where coral shrimp from the shelter of their caves wave their claws and antennae at the outside world. This is probably a signal to various reef fish to come and be cleaned. Here a sea horse (*Hippocampus sp.*) allows itself to be cleaned by a banded coral shrimp (*Stenopus hispidus*).*

◀ *The cleaner shrimp (*Lysmata amboinensis*) is a veritable invertebrate dermatologist but if it has no tankmates to groom, it will look elsewhere for food. Here the minuscule remains of several meals being picked at on the stem of a leather coral (*Sarcophyton sp.*). Lysmata grabhami, *a species that resembles* Lysmata amboinensis *very closely, can be recognized by the color pattern on its tail. This small detail aside, these two shrimps are effectively identical in appearance.*

◀ *Of all the known types of algae, the most abundant are the* Rhodophyta *(red algae) and the* Chlorophyta *(green algae). The sea cactus (*Halimeda sp.*) is a green alga that requires regular fertilization with calcium for normal growth. It is thus suitable only for the tanks of conscientious aquarists. The calcareous skeletons of these coraline algae, along with the feces of parrotfish, contribute to a reef's layer of sediment.*

▼ *While the Family* Caulerpacae *comprises only one genus,* Caulerpa, *that genus is rich in species; 75 have been described, a figure that does not include numerous morphological varieties. Many* Caulerpa *species are notably polymorphic, the shape of their "leaves" changing when they are moved from one aquarium to another. Its adaptability and the rapidity with which it sends out new stolons have made it popular among hobbyists. A dozen species, with "leaves" shaped like feathers, marbles, or a knife blade, as in this* Caulerpa prolifera, *are available to hobbyists.*

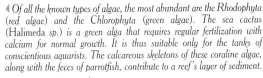
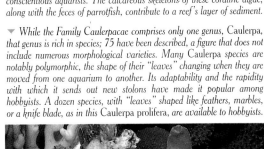

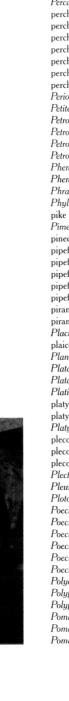

Glossary

Biotope: a habitat and the diverse physico-chemical and biological parameters one encounters therein, interacting to form a community of living creatures.

Chorion: the membrane that surrounds a developing embryo.

Endemic: a species whose geographic distribution is restricted to a single locality.

Euryhaline: capable of tolerating extreme variations in salinity.

Hermahprodite: an individual with functional male and female reproductive organs.

Hybrid: an organism arising from the interbreeding of two different species, whether in nature or due to human intervention.

Mouthbrooding or Buccal Incubation: retention of the developing embryos within the mouth and throat by one or both parents [usually the female] for the duration of their developmental interval.

Oviduct: the tube through which eggs pass from the ovaries to the external environment.

Oviparous: egg-laying

Ovoviviparous: retention of the fertilized eggs within the female's body until hatching, at which point the well-developed young are expelled.

Pelagic: living in open water.

Planktivore: an animal that feeds on plankton, either animal [zooplankton] or vegetable [phytoplankton].

Osmotic Pressure: force due to the difference in the concentration of dissolved substances on either side of a semi-permeable membrane.

Rheophile: an organism that lives in flowing water.

Sexual Dichromatism: differences in color between the male and female of the same species.

Sexual Dimorphism: differences in size and shape between male and female of the same species.

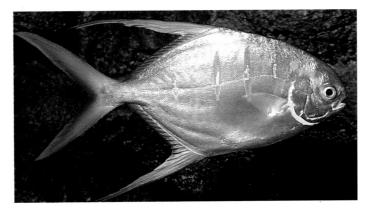

Sperm Duct: the tube through which sperm passes from the testes to the external environment.

Substratum: the surface upon which an organism lives.

Symbiosis: any association between two organisms.

Taxon: any recognized grouping of organisms.

Swim Bladder: a gas-filled structure that serves to maintain hydrostatic balance in most fish.

Viviparous: animals that retain the developing embryos within the body of the female, who nourishes them throughout their development, at the end of which they are expelled into the environment.

Captions

Cover photos, from left to right and from top to bottom:
Cover photo 1:
Pterophyllum scalare, Symphysodon aequifasciatus var. pigeon blood, *Betta splendens, Barbus tetrazona, Hemichromis* sp., *Poecilia reticulata, Pomacanthus maculosus, Paracheirodon axelrodi, Scorpaena scrofa.* Center: *Papiliochromis ramirezi.*
Cover photo 4:
Neolamprologus leleupi, Pseudochromis paccagnellae, Hippocampus sp., *Philipnodon* sp., *Carassius auratus, Aequidens rivulatus, Melanotaenia herbertaxelrodi, Scorpanea porcus, Aulonocara* hybrid, *Corydoras aeneus, Hypancistrus zebra, Pomacanthus paru, Raja clavata.* Center: *Pterois* complex *volitans.*

Large photo opposite the Contents:
Symphysodon aequifasciatius var. pigeon blood.

Opening pages for each chapter:
p. 4–5: *Betta splendens;* p. 12–13: *Paracheirodon axelrodi;* p. 34–35: *Brochis britskii;* p 42–43: *Hemichromis* sp.; p. 56–57: *Carassius auratus* telescope; p. 64–65: *Periophthalmus papilio;* p. 70–71: *Aspitrigla cucula;* p. 82–83: *Holacanthus ciliaris;* p. 108–109: *Taenianotus triacanthus.*

Index photos
p. 122: *Holacanthus bermudensis;* p. 123: top, *Macropodus ocellatus,* bottom, *Xiphophorus helleri;* p. 124: *Tilapia mariae.*
p. 125: *Sciaenochromis fryeri;* p. 126: *Bodianus anthioides;* p. 127: top, *Centropyge heraldi,* bottom *Trachinodus goodei.*

Photo Credits

All photos from the agency Aqua Press, 24140 Saint-Julien-de-Crempse.
Most of the photos were taken by Marie-Paule and Christian Piednoir. The others were by:
Marc Biehler: p. 95 (*Pomacanthus arcuatus*), p. 103 (*Epinephelus tukula, Epinephelus multinotatus*), p. 107 (*Orectolobus ornatus*), p. 111 (*Scorpaenopsis oxycephala*), p. 113 (*Diodon hystrix*), p. 114 (*Gymnothorax javanicus*), p. 116 (*Cheilinus undulatus*), p. 117 (*Cantherines macrocerus*); Jean-Marc Bour: p. 113 (*Diodon liturosus*); Maurice Chauche: p. 6 (*Betta brownorum*), p. 28 (*Cynolebias fulminantis*), p. 29 (*Aphyosemion ogoense* pyrophore, *Aphyosemion australe*); Michel Dune: p. 90 (*Chaetodon semilarvatus*), p. 98 (*Bodianus anthioides*), p. 101 (*Cheilinus undulatus, Thalassoma klunzigeri*), p. 104 (*Balistapus undulatus*), p. 107 (*Priacanthus hamrur*), p. 113 (*Arothron diadematus*), p. 114 (*Gymnothorax nudivomer*), p. 115 (*Corythoichthys flavofasciatus*), p. 116 (*Tacniura lymna, Pardachirus marmoratus*), p. 117 (female *Scarus gibbus*); Patrice Francour: p. 63 (*Ictalurus melas*), p. 74 (*Mullus surmuletus*), p. 76 (*Symphodus ocellatus*), p. 79 (*Dentex dentex*); Jean-Pierre Hacard: p. 55 (Lake Victoria, fisherman and *Lates niloticus*); Sylvie Houtmann: p. 78 (*Diplodus vulgaris*), p. 103 (*Hypoplectus unicolor guttavarius*), p. 107 (*Plectorhinchus orientalis*), p. 113 (*Arothron mappa*); Jean-Marie Londiveau: p. 52 (Malawi fisherman, *Tyranochromis* sp.); Steven Weinberg: p. 72 (*Tripterygion xanthosoma, Tripterygion tripteronotus, Parablennius gattorugine, Parablennius rouxi*), p. 73 (*Blennius incognitus, Lepadogaster lepadogaster, Scophtalmus rhombus*), p. 79 (*Scorpaena notata*), p. 81 (*Hippocampus ramulosus, Conger conger*), p. 84 (*Bryaenops youngei, Bryaenops amplus*), p. 87 (*Amphiprion nigripes, Premnas biaculeatus*), p. 111 (*Ablabys taenianotus, Scorpaenopsis diabolus, Scorpaenopsis venosa*), p. 117 (male *Scarus gibbus*), p. 120 (*Amphiprion nigripes*).

Acknowledgments

For their warmth, their help, and their friendship for many years, the authors wish to thank:
the directors and biologists of the public aquaria, Aquarélite, Aquamadern, Exomarc, Guinéa, Haegel, Koï Service, Lagon Import, Pisiculture of Estalens, Animal Planet, Huet and Tropica aquaculture station, and the photo divers who, by sharing our common passion, helped develop this work.

Original title: *Les Poissons d'Aquarium en 1000 Photos.*
© Copyright 1998 by Copyright Studio, Paris, France.
English-language edition © Copyright 2000 by Barron's Educational Series, Inc.

All inquiries should be addressed to:
Barron's Educational Series, Inc.
250 Wireless Boulevard
Hauppauge, New York 11788
http://www.barronseduc.com

Library of Congress Catalog Card No.: 99-72125

International Standard Book No. 0-7641-5217-3

PRINTED IN SPAIN
9 8 7 6 5 4 3 2 1